Praise for *Sport Matters*

"In *Sport Matters*, Kenneth L. Shropshire shines a light on recent sports controversies that show us how far we have to go to create a culture of respect and civility in sport. Fortunately, he also recommends steps toward making important changes, which we hope will lead to true progress. Highly recommended for anyone who wants to understand the critical leadership challenges in sports today."
—**Stephen M. Ross, Owner, Miami Dolphins**

"There has been significant social change over the years, but as Kenneth L. Shropshire argues in *Sport Matters*, the power and money are still not available to all, regardless of gender, race, and sexual orientation. Shropshire shows how we can make deeper progress toward leveling the playing field."
—**Billie Jean King, Former World #1 Tennis Champion and Activist**

"Kenneth L. Shropshire's *Sport Matters* is nothing short of essential reading. In a diverse society, each individual should enjoy the respect and equal access to which they are entitled, regardless of their race or any other aspect of their background. As Shropshire notes, this is still not a reality within the world of sports. In *Sport Matters*, Shropshire points the way forward. This book should be read by all of those who are interested in, or even curious about, sports."
—**Charles J. Ogletree, Jr., Harvard Law School Jesse Climenko Professor of Law and author of more than one dozen books**

"*Sport Matters* makes a seminal contribution to our understa   f the power structures, roles, and broader societal contexts and the American sports enterprise today. Professor Kenneth firsthand knowledge and insights, born of years of expe and consulting with sports leagues, teams, and individu combined with the keen analytical and deconstruct   practicing attorney, uniquely positions him to explore   .al connections and relationships between development   nd the sports arena. A must read for all who are seriou   ..the consequences of sport in America today."
—**Harry Edwards, PhD, Professor Emeritus, University of C   rnia, Berkeley, and Consultant, National Football League and National Basketball Association**

"The concerns and solutions set forth in *Sport Matters* are invaluable for those focused on improving sport and its impact around the globe."
—**Mori Taheripour, Former Senior Advisor, Sport for Development, US Agency for International Development (USAID)**

"In *Sport Matters*, Kenneth L. Shropshire examines several troubling controversies in sports that stem from a persistent lack of diversity, inclusion, respect, and equality. But Shropshire offers ways to address these challenges and attests to sport's ability to combat racial, gender, and social inequities in sports and throughout society. It is a must read for anyone who wishes to see sports as a means for social change."
—**Richard E. Lapchick, Chair, DeVos Sport Business Management Program, University of Central Florida, and Director, Institute for Diversity and Ethics in Sport**

"*Sport Matters* confirms that Ken Shropshire is the nation's most thoughtful and incisive voice on issues of sport and society. In the book, Shropshire examines a number of challenges and societal ills with which the sports world is currently grappling—from racial disparagement to domestic violence to homophobia to questions of exploitation in collegiate athletics—and puts them in solid historical context while challenging us to consider how the future could and should look. It is a brilliant exploration and a must read for anyone who questions what sport means to our society."
—**N. Jeremi Duru, Law Professor, American University, and Author, *Advancing the Ball: Race, Reformation, and the Quest for Equal Coaching Opportunity in the NFL***

"Kenneth L. Shropshire's *Sport Matters* reminds us that diversity and inclusion strengthen and enrich us all. The book is highly recommended for those who wish to understand the need for respect in the world of sports and beyond."
—**Patrick T. Harker, President, University of Delaware**

SPORT MATTERS

Leadership, Power, and the Quest for Respect in Sports

KENNETH L. SHROPSHIRE

WHARTON
SCHOOL
PRESS

Philadelphia

© 2014 by Kenneth L. Shropshire

Published by Wharton School Press
The Wharton School
University of Pennsylvania
3620 Locust Walk
2000 Steinberg Hall–Dietrich Hall
Philadelphia, PA 19104
Email: whartonschoolpress@wharton.upenn.edu
Website: wsp.wharton.upenn.edu

Ebook ISBN: 978-1-61363-050-1
Paperback ISBN: 978-1-61363-051-8

Please contact Wharton School Press for special discounts on bulk purchases
of ebooks and paperbacks: whartonschoolpress@wharton.upenn.edu

Contents

Preface
Of the Meaning of Progress

"Although there is no progress without change, not all change
is progress."
—John Wooden, *Wooden: A Lifetime of Observations
and Reflections On and Off the Court*[1]

In 1908, my great-aunt Bess Bolden Walcott was hired by Booker
T. Washington to organize his library at what was then called the
Tuskegee Industrial and Normal Institute.[2] Nearly 80 years later, on
the occasion of her 100th birthday, I joined my extended family in
gathering at Aunt Bess's home in Tuskegee, Alabama, to celebrate.
We all maneuvered around the room in hopes of getting a word
of wisdom from our matriarch before we took communion. I had
just been a professor at The Wharton School at the University of
Pennsylvania for a few months by then, and I may have projected
that I was a tad full of myself.

Aunt Bess was having none of it. This was a woman, after all,
who had traveled the world—and a woman who in my youth had
sent me invaluable information for my school papers, including
what I considered to be my fourth-grade masterpiece on George
Washington Carver, the African American scientist (and another
senior colleague of hers) who did the unimaginable with the peanut.
I was next in line.

"So you," she said, "are the *writer*." At some point as a little kid I
had made that pronouncement, having moved on from my previous

1

ambitions to have a career as a fireman or veterinarian. It was a small remark but a pointed one; Aunt Bess was both reminding and anointing. There was a room full of family waiting for their turn, but as I looked at that long gray hair and that miraculously intricately wrinkled face—one in which I could see both my mother and grandmother—she opened her eyes a bit wider and offered some simple yet powerful advice. "Don't be a bump on a log." And then Aunt Bess was done. She looked away and motioned on to the next family member.

I had only talked about writing books up until that point. After leaving Aunt Bess that day, I decided it was time to finally get to work. Among the books I would write over the next decade was one titled *In Black and White: Race and Sports in America*.[3] No bump on a log was I to be. The major focus of the book was on the absence of African Americans in power positions in sports. It was an important work, and I remain proud of it today.

What some point to as the principal shortcoming of that work is right there in the title—the exclusive focus on black and white. In my defense, however, it must be noted that the focus of that book actually was on blacks and whites, to the exclusion of other racial and ethnic groups, and it focused only on race issues in the United States. That brings us to this present effort to get off that log and to examine the issue as it has evolved.

Where Are We Today?

The media has brought global attention to several recent sports controversies that include issues of race but extend far beyond it. The Donald Sterling racial rant, the so-called bullying case in Miami, the use of the name *Redskins*, the assault on the National Collegiate Athletic Association (NCAA), and the myriad of dynamics in the Ray Rice case highlight just a few of those issues.

Today, rather than simply "black versus white," *diversity* is the watchword, and its ready copilot is "inclusion," a notion that is every bit as complicated. Diversity describes differences between people, however those differences are defined, whether by race, ethnicity, socioeconomic status, gender, sexual orientation, ability, or any other aspect of a person's background. Inclusion is actually bringing diversity into the enterprise in a meaningful way. Merely having individuals from different backgrounds and perspectives is not enough. While still not losing sight of the plight of North American and particularly US-based descendants of slaves, I embrace the broader goal of respect and equality in sports and beyond, a state I feel can only, and with great difficulty, be achieved through diversity and inclusion.

As US Attorney General Eric Holder asserted in calling us all cowards, I believe we have difficulty, as a country, discussing race. For whatever it does to accelerate the conversation, I contend that we can all talk about respect and what that entails. *Respect* is a word that resonates from the highest halls of power, to which The Wharton School has provided me entrée today, all the way back to the Crenshaw District in Los Angeles, where I grew up. In the broadest sense I have concluded that much of what all of us seek for ourselves and others is simple respect. I have found defining respect to be more complicated than I had imagined. Certainly it is about how we treat each other. But even more nuanced, it is about how we *believe* we should be treated. We hear a lot today, for example, about microaggressions, the smallest measures of disrespect that many do not notice and that others indicate that it is absurd for us to notice.[5] This smallest level and the nuance of how each individual wants to be treated, and believes he or she should be treated, is where we need to focus.[6]

Thanks to my role as a consultant, a lawyer, and director of the Wharton Sports Business Initiative, and my work as the David W. Hauck Professor of legal studies and business ethics and Africana studies, I have had the opportunity to examine these issues—live these issues, really—up close and in person, and these experiences have given me both a fuller understanding of just how immense these problems are and how great an impact the world of sports can make when the right decisions are made by those in positions of power. I have consulted with the National Football League (NFL), Major League Baseball, the NCAA, other top sports organizations, owners, executives, and athletes for years on issues often related to diversity and inclusion, and, without always labeling it as such, equality and respect. For example, I have been working with Stephen Ross, owner of the Miami Dolphins, as a consultant to establish an initiative focused on issues of equality, respect, diversity, and inclusion. He has experienced a combination of these issues with his franchise that I will cover later in this book. As Ross said to me in our initial conversation about some of these very issues, "It's about race," he said, "but it's not all about race." That point is an important one, and one I take to heart in this book. This work examines issues that go far beyond black and white.

The focus of this book is on the unique leadership challenge to embrace and deliver these principles in a real and tangible way within the sports industry specifically. The book is intended to be a snapshot of where we stand in our societal journey by focusing on the key sports power issues of the day. It also seeks to provide business and other leadership lessons and the outline of a framework that can be applied beyond the world of sports. In this work, I use examples from the United States. The global issues of bananas on soccer pitches, the broader issues of the global participation in sport by women, and the gender questions raised regarding athletes such as Caster Semenya in South Africa would lead us to yet another layer of complexity in this discussion.[7] If the focus of this work were on the composition of players, the global issues would be extraordinarily important, especially regarding the decline in the number of African Americans playing Major League Baseball. It is relevant, however, that as the global economy has evolved, the likes of Russian Mikhail Prokhorov can purchase a National Basketball Association (NBA) franchise while African Americans and Latinos generally remain on the ownership sidelines.[8]

In the introduction, I describe the Sports Power Matrix, a basic framework for understanding power within the sports industry. In the chapters that follow, I explore the sports controversies that have captured headlines as a prism for exploring diversity, inclusion, respect, and equality in sports. Of course, innumerable other possible topics could have been used as a prism, and I am not proclaiming those addressed in this book to be the only issues that are relevant. In fact, as I have found, the relevant topics of a given day will most often evolve over time.[9] We can only hope that progress is achieved. But I caution that if that is to happen, there is much work to be done. The nature of the format of this work allows for a highlighting of the issues and a framework for focus if not the depth of analysis that must take place going forward.

We Are Not Postracial

Some readers may believe that I should set a foundation regarding the broader climate on diversity before examining the issues specific to sport. On the topic of race, for example, some people express an optimism, particularly following the election of Barack Obama in 2008, that we are somehow in a postracial society. Such a discussion, defining the status of race relations and diversity today, would constitute a separate work in itself. I do want to state, clearly, that we are not in a postracial society and that problems of race still lead as a societal concern. In this work, I am building off the landscape I defined in *In Black and White: Race and Sports in America*. There I devoted a great deal of space to the plight of African Americans and the long history of discrimination and exclusion in sports. Because this is, in a sense, an extension of that earlier work, I intentionally give short shrift to providing the extensive foundation that some readers may desire. For those who do want a deeper background, that work and certainly many others would provide a base. For context, in that earlier book, I led with a discussion of the Rodney King case, the differing racial reactions to the O. J. Simpson verdict, and the use of the Willie Horton advertisement in George H. W. Bush's campaign against Democratic candidate Michael Dukakis. Today I could lead similarly with the racial unrest in Ferguson, Missouri, related to the killing of Michael Brown; the killing of Eric Garner and the "I can't breathe" protests that followed; the case of George Zimmerman in the killing of Trayvon Martin; or even my own handcuffing in a Philadelphia suburb as an accused bank robber. But here I leave it to the reader to reflect more broadly on the racial context of today, and I ask that you also reflect on the broader issues confronting society beyond the dominant racial issues. Here, I focus on where we are today in the narrow but far-reaching realm of sports. One need only pick up a copy of the *SportsBusiness Journal* and look at the faces in issues featuring the most powerful or influential people in sport or examine the photos of industry leaders speaking at a given upcoming conference to see that white males typically dominate those pages disproportionately, contrary to the imagery of the players on the field of play.[10]

On Progress

"Of the Meaning of Progress" is the title of a particularly powerful chapter in W. E. B. DuBois's timeless work *The Souls of Black Folks*.[11] There, arguably the most influential African American thinker of all time reflects on his return to the poor black schools in rural Tennessee in which he had taught several years before. He ruminates on how things have changed and searches for "progress." Note the distinction raised here, between change and progress. That distinction is raised in the epigraph by John Wooden at the start of this preface and has also been highlighted to me by Dr. Harry Edwards, Professor Emeritus of Sociology at the University of California, Berkeley, one of my key mentors. Change, or modest difference, does not validate the existence of progress. And DuBois does find change—but then ends the chapter by writing that he was forced to make his way home in a segregated "Jim Crow" railcar. It makes for an abrupt but undeniably powerful ending to a chapter that had been sprinkled with some hope. My point of sharing this anecdote is this: When I look at sport today, relative to my earliest ruminations on the subject all of those years ago, I can't help but think of DuBois's "Of the Meaning of Progress"—the good, yes, but also the tragically bad. Change has occurred, but disturbingly little progress has been made where it really counts.

If we look at the often incredibly powerful impact sport has had on our culture over the past century, we should be concerned— deeply concerned, I think—if sport does not continue to provide the positive societal impact and imagery we have seen from the likes of Joe Louis, Jesse Owens, Billie Jean King, and of course Jackie Robinson, not to mention Muhammad Ali. But the next step has to be a reality of greater diversity beyond the field of play, with the greater access to power that it brings.

Can we really even begin to aspire to a world beyond *just* diversity? Well, yes, what we all want is basic respect and equality— though as we will learn shortly, these things are not easy to achieve. They are worth striving for, however. Thus the four key concerns of this book—diversity, inclusion, respect, and equality—are the massively important principles that drive the discussion herein. If we can collectively focus on fully adopting and incorporating these principles, we can avoid the potentially dire consequences. With a nod to the double entendre at the heart of *Race Matters*,[12] Dr. Cornel West's great work, I offer up *Sport Matters*, triple entendre intended, to delve into these issues.

Introduction
The Sports Power Matrix

When Clippers owner Donald Sterling went on a racist rant, sponsors began distancing themselves from him immediately. That is the result in some of the cases I explore in this book. When sponsors feel a team, owner, or player they have supported harms their brand, they withdraw their sponsorship, a direct hit to the bottom line.

But beyond dropped sponsors or lower ticket sales from angry fans, what is the business case for a leadership focus on diversity, inclusion, respect, and equality? Roger Goodell, National Football League (NFL) commissioner, helps us get closer to the answer in a report focused on coaching mobility in the NFL:

> Bringing together people with diverse racial, ethnic and gender backgrounds provides far-reaching and varied perspectives and skills that are crucial for any organization to expand its horizons. Making diversity in the workplace a priority is good business. A collaborative and inclusive team of employees provides the foundation for success and growth and we believe in it strongly.[13]

Often, the conversation about diversity in business focuses on whether the expenditures to support diversity initiatives are good for the company's bottom line. However, tracking measurable revenues from diversity programs has proven to be difficult.

While some studies in this area show the positive impact of the announcement of a diversity program on the market price of that company's stock, any evidence that these principles are good for business is fuzzy at best.[14] Certainly, if you can bring in a broader sector of society as clients or customers, that's a good thing. If your company has everyone getting along and acting respectfully, more is likely to get done. But splicing data to peg success to greater adherence to these four principles has always struck me as time wasted. In the end, if diversity, inclusion, respect, and equality do not impact the bottom line, is that really good enough reason to move away from them or to view them as not *good business*?

The Power of Sports in Society

In *Take Time for Paradise*,[15] the late Major League Baseball commissioner and Yale University president A. Bartlett Giamatti wrote that we can learn much more about a society by watching how it plays than how it works. Giamatti's theme reveals the importance of sport beyond sport and why sport matters. His eloquence in that work serves as an excellent foundation for using sport to contemplate issues beyond the games themselves. Giamatti had it only partially right. The "why" we play is also a question worth pondering. Why we let the games we play and watch influence us beyond who wins and loses is a question constantly explored, too.

With much that is good and powerful about the imagery of sport bringing people together, what issues remain problematic? Where is there still an absence of respect, equality, and inclusion, even where we see diversity? These questions provide a basic framework on which we can begin to compartmentalize this massive sports issue.

Examining and acknowledging the changes we have seen is merely part of the process of facing the reality of where we are and how much further we have to go. This reminds me of Jim Collins, in *Good to Great*, citing the Stockdale Paradox: "You must retain faith that you will prevail in the end and you must also confront the most brutal facts of your current reality."[16] That quote comes from

Admiral James Stockdale, reflecting on his time as a prisoner of war in Vietnam, offering us a sort of mantra for difficult or seemingly impossible situations. Stockdale had to believe that one day he would get out, but he also had to accept that the circumstances he was in were unbearable—and that little hope was actually present day to day. The Stockdale quote is only partly relevant here. I love the optimism. But we also must make a clear distinction: Stockdale knew that rescue and escape were solutions to his reality. We do not know what solution exists to end racism or even if a solution exists. Where we can all envision a *Rambo* moment saving prisoners of war, who or what will save us from racism is a mystery we continue to confront, no matter how optimistic we are. This is a major part of the difficulty in focusing on this issue: there is no universal event that will propel us to "prevailing" over the issues discussed herein.

Which brings me back to the world of sports. When I mention to people my dream of bringing about diversity, inclusion, respect, and equality in sport, I often hear a version of this: "Good luck with that. Why don't you aim for solving world hunger and poverty while you are at it?" It is a massive task to comprehend, and of course I understand that. But it is one we should believe we can take on.

On the field of play, decades ago, few foresaw the success of Venus and Serena Williams in the largely white, country club sport of tennis. Or could they? We know that decades before them, African Americans Althea Gibson and Arthur Ashe both won major tennis tournaments in much more racially oppressive times. These are individual athletic accomplishments. We are also seeing an all-time high number of black quarterbacks in the National Football League; even 20 years ago, this seemed improbable—but not necessarily so to football insiders who began to look for anyone who could evade the rush of the likes of Lawrence Taylor. Change came about as rigid color barriers fell and necessity dictated a style that could bring about on-field success. This increasing diversity of athletes is a part of the *good* of the current reality. What is the bad, at least in the context of this book? My primary focus is on the business side of sports, rather than the field of play. Yes, the success and composition of players who are "different" in some respect in the games is worthy of commentary, but the questions that I am more interested in, and that we should all be more interested in, are the following: Where are we in sports as they relate to money and control? Who holds the power beyond the field of play? If we look even more closely, are we living in a time of true equality, respect, and inclusion? And how do we improve the situation we presently have? In that respect, Venus, Serena, and multiple black quarterbacks mean very little if anything at all.

The Sports Power Matrix

To analyze these issues I'll frame much of the discussion using a matrix that captures the key power parties in sports related to diversity, inclusion, respect, and equality. It is a simple model, but I ask the reader to conceptualize power in sports as a matrix divided into multiple segments: a pie divided into relevant-sized slices. Envision these segments being of varying sizes related to their relative powers. The power of each segment will be discussed throughout. Note, too, that the power of each sector may vary depending on the circumstances. For example, a player's union with the will to strike is much more powerful than one without that will. Or, as will be discussed, extraordinary power was exerted by the players in resolving the Donald Sterling matter. Owners, managers, and athletes will be the primary focus. These three segments represent the major day-to-day participants in the industry. However, I will note multiple other segments throughout. These include the external parties: vendors, suppliers, sponsors, fans, media, and even governmental entities such as the courts. The power of these segments can be tremendous. If the media chose, for example, not to broadcast the games, that would be extraordinarily powerful. These segments, as they relate to the issues in this book, are relatively self-explanatory. For clarity's sake, however, within the management segment I include those at league and administrative offices, such as league commissioners, and leaders of entities such as the International Olympic Committee and the NCAA.

Figure 1: Sports Power Matrix

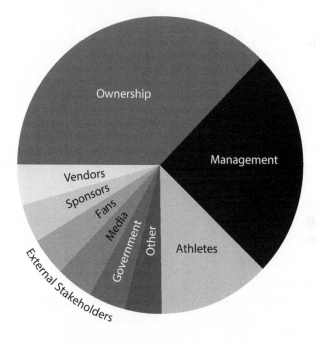

The segment sizes are for illustrative purposes. The dynamics in power are not static. Each segment's power expands and contracts depending on the circumstances.

Progress vs. Change?

There has been undeniable change since the publication of *In Black and White*. For example, if we look at the true power positions in US sports, there is one Latino majority franchise owner in Major League Baseball and one African American majority franchise owner in the NBA.[17] In 1996, the year *In Black and White* was published, there were none. I submit that that small increase is change. Certainly not celebratory progress. The question must be asked: are "broken" barriers merely illusory when it comes to *real* progress? To answer that, we need to look to the past—and the present.

We have entered a new phase in our societal efforts toward diversity and inclusion. In sports, no matter how many more objective measures are used to determine who plays, the opportunity remains for subjective decisions made with regard to race, sexual orientation, and other differences. In one sense, diversity is nearly universally present, at least on the fields of play in the United States. Regarding head coach, general manager, and team president jobs, however, decisions about who gets what role go far beyond the objective. Where subjectivity is allowed in an even broader way than on the field of play, both conscious and unconscious discrimination continue to occur.

At this highest level—the continued lack of diversity in the ownership segment of the Sports Power Matrix—is one of those sport-and-beyond issues based more on the economics of African Americans overall, not specifically related to sport. And while this book will explore the nuances of many of the segments, much of our attention will focus on the ownership segment. The reason, of course, is simple: without diversity at the highest leadership levels in sports—in terms of race, gender, outlook, and other factors—decisions that reflect and support true respect and inclusion will be difficult if not impossible to achieve.

Sustaining Change to Achieve Progress: The Rooney Rule

Change is undeniable, but problems continue, and those problems—the challenges we face both in and out of sports—only grow more difficult over time and real progress is not allowed to take hold. Indeed, many questions must be asked: At the highest levels in and out of sport, in what instances (and how) have issues of diversity been successfully addressed? Once diversity in numbers does occur, how is inclusiveness achieved? How are "newcomers" brought into the lifeblood of the activity of an organization, especially if they are "different"? Is there assurance that these individuals are treated equally and with respect?

Part of what we see in sports, as with society as a whole, is inconsistent change that is not sustained. For example, in the NFL, more African Americans have been hired for head coaching positions; that much is undeniable. Yet during the 2013 NFL hiring season, with over a dozen openings available, not a single African American was hired as a head coach or general manager. After so much change, progress could not be achieved and sustained. Clearly, what was being done was a piece of the puzzle, but multiple pieces are required in order to sustain the effort.

Notably, hiring changes in the NFL began only after the implementation of the so-called Rooney Rule. This rule, named after legendary Pittsburgh Steelers owner Dan Rooney and implemented in 2003, requires all NFL teams to interview at least one nonwhite candidate for head coaching jobs. Since the rule was put in place, 17 teams have had at least one African American or Latino head coach. Three of the league's 32 teams have had more than one. That is a dramatic change. If sustained, it would have represented progress.[18]

The rule came about following research conducted by University of Pennsylvania professor Janice Madden that showed that even with *better* coaching records, African American head coaches in the NFL retained and obtained jobs at a lower rate than their white counterparts with lesser records.[19] Following the publication of this report, legendary civil rights attorneys Johnnie Cochran and Cyrus Mehri threatened lawsuits against the league if change did not occur. Thus came the implementation of the Rooney Rule. More recently, the NFL, after seeing change slow, has been proactive in reinstituting a more systematic approach that had brought about the initial waves of progress. Not surprisingly, the change came. They began hosting a career symposium for prospective coaches and front office executives. At this multiday gathering the prospects meet decision makers, including owners in both formal and informal settings; a high percentage of attendees over the past two years have obtained jobs in the hiring season following attending.[20] This NFL Career Development Symposium was a recycling, of sorts, of a program first implemented by the late NFL head coach Bill Walsh and Dr. Harry Edwards in 1986. This program was based on the simple principle of providing networking opportunities and instruction on getting the key jobs that did not naturally occur. Again, these are pieces of the puzzle, but the additional pieces must continue to be sought and sustained. If this change can be maintained, that will constitute progress.

This is a great place to reflect on the possibility of instilling these equity issues in youth and school sports programs at the earliest stages, not only by what lessons we deliver to kids on a formal basis, but by reviewing the diversity of the local Pop Warner or Little League baseball administration. In short, in the *Paradise* that Giamatti describes, it is never too early to focus on the issues addressed in this book.

Achieving the Goal

Management and personal success books make it clear that a goal without a plan is a wish. As a kid I waited, naïvely, for integration to arrive—a philosophy that my child's mind told me would end the race problems that appeared on my nightly news. In *In Black and White*, I wrote that ownership by people of color was a majestic moment that would move us dramatically forward. Perhaps what I really meant at the time was that the chances of ownership by African Americans and Latinos were so remote that such a miracle would serve as the canary in the race and sports mine—that once it died, so too would racism. That canary is still with us.

With laws in place barring discrimination, what can we do, beyond awaiting the passage of time, to bring about change and greater diversity, inclusion, respect, and equality? One short-term goal is a plan that brings about change and is sustainable. The development of that plan or, as will be discussed, multiple plans, even where willingness exists, has been difficult. The Rooney Rule and NFL Career Development Symposiums—their successes and failures—are examples of the level of vigilance required.

W. E. B. DuBois in the early 1900s called the "race problem" the biggest challenge facing the United States in the twentieth century. Sadly but perhaps predictably, the great historian John Hope Franklin placed that same tag on the twenty-first century 90 years later. As Franklin wrote in 1993: "Without any pretense of originality or prescience, with less than a decade left in this century, I venture to state categorically that the problem of the twenty-first century will be the problem of the color line. This conclusion arises from the fact that by any standard of measurement or evaluation the problem has not been solved in the twentieth century, and this becomes a part of the legacy and burden of the next century. Consequently, it follows the pattern that the nineteenth century bequeathed to the twentieth century and that the eighteenth century handed to its successor."[21] Though not as dominant, the broad range of diversity, inclusion, respect, and equality issues beyond race were with us in the last century and continue with us in this century. Thus, a major part of this work is acknowledging the current state of affairs. Perhaps a more correct forecast by Franklin would have labeled diversity as the problem of the twenty-first century as well. The race issue will not be addressed in a vacuum but has a greater chance of being fully addressed in the context of diversity and respect.

Today we are pushed to conceptualize these issues within the frame of diversity. One could battle with this concept, and I for one have. But in this work I seek to look at this broader diversity issue while being relentless on the unique concerns related to race that cannot be ignored if solutions are ever to be found. Even as we acknowledge the challenge, however, we must listen to Stockdale; we must collectively believe we can "prevail in the end," even though in this journey we do not know definitively how the end may come about.

When will we have we arrived? What is the "perfect storm" of diversity, inclusion, respect, and equality success that will wash away the myriad problems that confront us in both sports and society? Let's explore where we are, contemplate whether we can ever reach such an unfathomable goal, and determine what actions and costs are required and what that goal will look like as a sustainable reality. When we get there. If we get there. At the risk of simplicity, as you read, reflect on seven key leadership lessons:

1. Diversity must be accompanied by inclusion.
2. Addressing these issues requires more than a single action or policy.
3. The actions or policies must be sustained.
4. Leadership must be vigilant regarding the need to revise policies.
5. Negative behavior must be responded to rapidly and decisively but with due process.
6. Race consciousness remains imperative.
7. Where possible, seek to have an impact beyond your enterprise.

This book intends to move us in this direction.

CHAPTER 1

An Imbalance of Power
*What the Donald Sterling Drama Can
Teach Us about Diversity and Inclusion*

You can sleep with [black people]. You can bring them in, you
can do whatever you want. The little I ask you is not to promote
it on [Instagram] . . . and not to bring them to my games." With those
words to V. Stiviano, a female friend of his who reportedly identifies
as black and Mexican and whom the media called his then-girlfriend,
former Los Angeles Clippers owner Donald Sterling sealed his fate.[22]

The focus of Sterling's rampage that day—a rampage that would
eventually result in his ouster from the NBA—was black people in
the form of Magic Johnson, the former Los Angeles Lakers great and
accomplished businessman. Stiviano had posted images of Johnson
on her Instagram account. Sterling did not approve. Because Magic
Johnson is black. "Don't put [Magic] on an Instagram for the world
to have to see, so they have to call me," Sterling was recorded saying.
"And don't bring him to my games."[23] The complicated totality of
this was that Sterling was directing this toward all black people, not
just Magic. Sterling's past allowed us to translate "don't bring *him*" to
"don't bring *them*."

At its most basic level, this commentary was simply and starkly
racist. There is no denying that. But a closer examination of Sterling's
tirade can lead us to a greater understanding of the relative absence
of—and the need for—diversity and inclusion within the ownership
segment of the Sports Power Matrix.

Concern about diversity often originates with the statistics—
how well or how poorly a given group is represented within an
organization. But inclusion is the *qualitative* side of the coin: how
well does an organization incorporate individuals from a variety
of backgrounds into every segment of its operation and being? The
important takeaway here—the one lesson that I think the Sterling
matter drives home most forcibly—is that an organization can be
mathematically diverse and at the same time *noninclusive*. That's
because inclusion is more difficult to achieve than diversity. In the
Clippers setting, diversity was present in the front office and on
the playing floor, but the leadership message was clearly not one of
inclusion. More starkly one can argue that on April 14, 1947, Major
League Baseball was segregated and then on April 15, 1947, Major
League Baseball was diverse. However, it was hardly inclusive.

The Illusion of Progress

Few who understand the sports business will argue against the
proposition that of the multiple segments in the Sports Power
Matrix, the most easily commanded and exercisable power rests
with ownership. Of course, it is also within this segment that we find
the lowest level of diversity.

Donald Sterling became the owner of the Clippers franchise
in 1981 by paying a mere $12.5 million[24]—"mere," relative to the
$2-billion-plus sum that was paid more recently for the Los Angeles
Dodgers and Sterling's own Clippers.[25] The significance of Sterling's
acquisition date and the price that he paid is that this was when the
window existed where economics would have allowed for African
American ownership. However, it simply did not happen. African
American franchise seekers showed the desire and made the effort,
but in that era only one African American ownership group had any
degree of success, with that group briefly owning a managing share
of the Denver Nuggets of the NBA from 1989 to 1992.[26]

In discussing ownership, it is always important to pause and reflect on the existence of professional sports enterprises owned by African Americans during the segregation era that ran until the early 1960s. The most dominant of these were collectively referred to as the Negro Leagues. At their peak, for example, the attendance numbers for the Chicago American Giants of the Negro Leagues exceeded that of the Cubs and the White Sox on any given Sunday. In short, this era of ownership by men, and in some cases women, who were descendants of slaves began to dwindle when integration occurred after Jackie Robinson broke the Major League Baseball color barrier in 1947. There is much that was unromantic about the Negro Leagues, from the facilities to travel conditions, but the level of black business control has not been present in sports since the destruction of the Negro Leagues by virtue of the integration of Major League Baseball in the middle of the last century.[27]

As for the Clippers, until recent years on the court the team has generally had little to celebrate, and from a strictly bottom-line point of view, many recognized the free-riding tactics of Sterling; the prevailing opinion among those close to the game was that he was simply in it for the money and never really had any interest in trying to put a winning team together. He spent little but rode the wave of financial success of the NBA at large. Franchise values continued to rise, and Sterling's investment proved to be a wise one.

The same could not be said for many of his other actions. Over the years, Sterling would make news in Los Angeles for things completely unrelated to the game of basketball. He faced lawsuits alleging discriminatory actions in his real estate business, and he also found himself at the wrong end of an age and race discrimination lawsuit filed by his longtime general manager, Elgin Baylor. Baylor, an African American, was also an NBA Hall of Fame player. Baylor was not successful in his suit.

As I have mentioned previously, in my early days of writing and thinking about this issue there were no African American ownership groups in any of the major American sports leagues. In *In Black and White*, I included a graphic that illustrated 100 percent white ownership across the NFL and NBA; I even included the National Hockey League (NHL), which has had Asian American ownership, and Major League Baseball, which was at 97 percent white ownership thanks only to an ownership stake by a resident of Japan. With that context in mind, I wrote about increased diversity in the ownership ranks as a piece of the solution to racism in sports. It wasn't so much naïveté about the potential impact of the presence of owners of color. Rather, I simply overestimated how greater diversity in the owners' suite would impact the day-to-day operations of the league.[29]

I envision the reality and symbolism of *big rooms* where decisions are made. They are big in the sense of power and in the sense of the size of the decisions. In *big rooms* with a person of color present, conversations are often forced to change, so that may well have occurred—in some ways. That is a piece of inclusiveness, to whatever extent it occurs in a given setting. But when the 30 or so other owners in a given league conduct their day-to-day business, if a diversity of views is not present *at their specific franchise*, that viewpoint may still be absent. The owners are not always in a *big room* where diversity is present. That can make all the difference.

In *Forty Million Dollar Slaves: The Rise, Fall, and Redemption of the Black Athlete*, William C. Rhoden tells the tale of how African American billionaire Bob Johnson managed to become the owner of the Charlotte Bobcats of the NBA. In that book, Rhoden explores the ownership record of Johnson, who made it a point to provide opportunities for African Americans in high-level positions. There was certainly a degree of symbolism in these efforts, but I don't think I'm understating things to say that Johnson's tenure represents only a mere blip on the sports diversity continuum. Like me, Rhoden believed for some time that the ownership moment would be what he called a sort of "Promised Land" for diversity in sports. It is clear to me now that changing the racial composition of ownership is just a small piece of the puzzle. Creating inclusion, by whatever means, is an even more important concern than the diversity brought by a single man or woman. Much more needs to occur. This inclusive process is the longer portion of the struggle. Rhoden summed it up with what ownership would have to represent in order to be meaningful: "Buying in is only the beginning; the key is to transform, to make something newer, fairer, more just. Something that responds to the demands of the chorus of history to create something new, to change the game."[30]

The power and distance that exists between billionaire sports franchise owners and those who watch (or play) the games may have been illustrated in the extreme in the Sterling case. The owner's ridiculous comments continue a trend line that has been with us since the post–civil rights era—a trend line that periodically brings to our attention the continuing problem of race in sports, no matter how diverse the field of play has become. And as the Sterling matter illustrated so powerfully, a major racial moment in sports can knock even the major story of the moment—in this instance, the search for a missing Malaysian airliner—out of the lead story slot in the nation's newspapers and television networks.

Sterling's words displayed a lack of respect to the majority of the men who make the NBA possible, and that sentiment gets right to the heart of what this book really means by "respect." Sterling's words indicate that he had a merely "tolerant relationship" with African Americans, and that's not good enough. The simple reality that we must accept, even in the face of perceived progress, is that little actual diversity exists in the seats of power in the world of sport. Because of that lack of diversity, true inclusion—and true respect—is simply not realistic. The power of ownership in sports is unique.

The Magic of Racial Exceptionalism: Degrees of Inclusion

The most obvious candidates to become African American franchise owners in Major League Baseball, the NFL, the NBA, or the NHL are three people known only by their first names—Magic, Michael, and Oprah—and, prospectively, any athlete currently playing in a major sports league, thereby accumulating the necessary capital to one day match the financial power of that trio. One must be extremely wealthy in order to be the lead member of an ownership group. Interestingly, Magic Johnson and Michael Jordan are both in the ownership ranks, and Oprah Winfrey recently bid to purchase the Los Angeles Clippers, and lost.

Magic is a black man and a former athlete with success at the highest levels in both sport and business, and in that sense he has proven that athletes can move on to greater success—and power. He found his way into ownership both in the NBA, having been a part owner of the Los Angeles Lakers, and in Major League Baseball, as a current member of the Los Angeles Dodgers ownership group. But he is also a former player from a lower socioeconomic background, and he does not hold the same kind of power that other owners do. Though Magic joins Michael Jordan (the Charlotte Hornets) and Arte Moreno (the Los Angeles Angels of Anaheim) as an African American or Latino owner in major American sports, he, unlike Jordan and Moreno, holds only a minority interest in the Dodgers.[31] Others, including African American businesswoman Sheila Johnson, have obtained minority ownership interests in the big four US-based leagues as well, with less fanfare than Magic. To be clear, there are other nonwhite owners today, which is a signal of greater diversity. These include Pakistan-born NFL Jacksonville Jaguars owner Shad Khan, Indian-born Sacramento Kings owner Vivek Ranadivé, and Moroccan-born Milwaukee Bucks owner Marc Lasry, who is geographically an African American.

Sheila Johnson is the first African American woman to be an owner or partner in three professional sports franchises: the Washington Capitals (NHL), the Washington Wizards (NBA), and the Washington Mystics (Women's National Basketball Association [WNBA]). She is exceptional in her own right, not simply because she is a multi-franchise-owning African American woman, but she is, like most owners, a business person and not a former super-athlete, as is the case with Magic and Michael. As for African Americans holding minority interests in sports, she is unique, too, in that she is not a former athlete or celebrity as are others who have held minority interests, including Magic, Shaquille O'Neal, Will Smith, Drake, Jay-Z, Usher, and Venus and Serena Williams.[32] But keep in mind that conceptually, if not in practice, at a meeting of owners within any league, there may only be 30 seats in the room—and 30 votes with no invitations extended to those with minority interests to cast an additional vote on league-wide decisions.[33]

That Magic, of all people, was the target of Sterling's rant was eye-opening. After all, whatever bias one might have against African Americans, and whatever stereotypes a racist mind might put upon them, Magic, one would think, would stand out as an exception to unreasonable hatred. Why would anyone have animus against this man who was outwardly so endearing and respected? The answer is more readily that this could have been directed at any black man; it just happened to be Magic.

In a subsequent interview with Anderson Cooper on CNN, Sterling tried to explain that he had problems with Magic because the former Laker had not done much for the black community. Of course, again, Magic was the wrong target here. Johnson has a history of business successes in urban communities, and in fact he built one of his Magic Johnson Theatres complexes in the Crenshaw Shopping Center, right in the neighborhood where I grew up. He was, and continues to be, an economic presence in these communities, in addition to being philanthropic. Sterling's rant made it clear that getting past race, no matter the accomplishments of the individual, is still a difficult task for some. That task appeared to be even more difficult for an out-of-touch billionaire. Some misguided souls likely saw Barack Obama winning the presidency of the United States as a sign that America has become "postracial"; the Sterling saga, however, was a sobering reminder of the progress that has yet to be achieved.

That's why "exceptionalisms" can be problematic. A Magic Johnson in an owner's suite. A Barack Obama in the Oval Office. A Ken Chenault leading American Express. A Meg Whitman excelling in corporate America. A Rick Welts serving as president of an NBA franchise. These exceptions raise the question, "They did it, why can't you?" These are great individual achievements, similar to the athletes mentioned earlier, and they have done their own part to increase "diversity"—at least by the numbers. But they cannot and do not add up to widespread diversity, inclusion, or respect. With the Sterling case, we saw an exceptional person of color being treated as negatively as any noncelebrity person of color. Magic had been singled out simply because of his race. And this made clear, for all to see, the dangerous power that an owner was able to assert simply because of his personal negative, racist views.

Sport as a Racial Lullaby

When the Sterling event hit the news, the media asked for my opinion. I was on NPR, CNN, and PBS and in the *New York Times* and other media, but the moment that stuck with me was just a brief exchange on a CNN special hosted by Don Lemon. I had the idea that sports had become sort of a lullaby regarding race—that some watch the games and see so much diversity on the field of play that we are lulled into a sense of believing that we have "arrived." The optics permit some to not examine any further where the *real* power is, or whether there is inclusion, equality, and respect. On the Lemon show, I took a little different course and referred to the dominance of people of color on the field as an "illusion." I did not invoke the full civil rights phrasing of "the *illusion of inclusion*,"[34] but I did refer to the dominance on the field by people of color as "*an illusion of progress.*"

Joining me on Lemon's show that day was criminal defense attorney Mark O'Mara—the same Mark O'Mara who had successfully defended George Zimmerman in the racially charged murder of African American youth Trayvon Martin in Florida. O'Mara, at least on one point, disagreed with my views. The relevant portions of the exchange are as follows:

> **Lemon:** . . . *Race permeates all aspects of our culture. . . . What is unique in the sports world?*

> **Shropshire:** . . . *[S]ports is a bit of an illusion that there's been this great amount of success. . . . You think of 1947, Jackie Robinson, the lone African American on the field. . . . Today . . . most of us don't know how many African Americans are playing. . . . Now it's the closer you get to the money. That's where African Americans . . . are absent. But that's not what we see on television. . . . sports provides this illusion of this great . . . progress, but it takes moments like [the Sterling case]. . . . for people to really understand that sports is like the rest of society. . . . the racial incidents are more clandestine, more undercover, but the racial prejudice is still there.*

> **Lemon:** . . . *I'm looking at the stats here . . . in 2013, African Americans comprised about 75 percent of all NBA players, 40 percent of all NBA head coaches, and certainly, a much smaller percentage of owners. So what dynamic does that cause?*

> **Shropshire:** . . . *[I]t's not too different from the rest of America . . . the numbers of people of color have been increased in a number of places in society. But when you look at the very top in sports, if you look at ownership, the absence is stark. And it's not so much that there's any special prejudice in sport. The economics don't allow people of color to participate at the highest levels. Now where there could be greater progress is at the president level, is at the CEO*

level, is at the head coaching level. And those are places where there's been modest progress, but we still have very strong evidence . . . that . . . issues that still permeate sports.

After I finished, there was some banter between Lemon and the other guests. I felt that even in that fleeting television moment, my point had been made. Then O'Mara chimed in.

O'Mara: I don't think you can call the progress we've made an illusion, however. We've made progress over the past 40 years, since . . . We just had—Jackie Robinson. But you can't say that that's an illusion. We still have a long way to go, but progress has been made, by the numbers that Don just talked about. We're just not there yet, and it's going to be a while to get there, but we are on our way.[35]

Then we were on to the next topic and I could not get my talking head back in to rebut. A sound bite would not provide the nuance needed to highlight change versus the progress O'Mara was proclaiming. In short, the illusion is that blacks and Latinos have power in sport because of the dominance on the field of play. But the owners make so much money that they can write the huge checks we hear about the players receiving on a daily basis. That is *real* power. Of course, the question is obvious: How do you make this highest level truly inclusive, absent an economic presence? How is a conscience brought into the ownership room? The economic impediment could keep us from overcoming the ownership diversity and inclusion barrier for some time. That much is undeniable.

But the other segments of the Sports Power Matrix can have an impact on this most powerful group and the decisions that they make. Owners must work to be inclusive, in whatever manner they can, or their insulation may lead to unequal and disrespectful decisions.

Management: Leading in the Face of Inequality

Commissioners of sports leagues are sometimes portrayed as the most powerful parties in this management segment, but they are actually a great deal less powerful than the owners. Largely, this is because commissioners typically work *for* the owners and can be fired by the owners (notably, none of the four major American sports leagues has ever been led by anyone other than a white male commissioner).

Although he was an NBA business veteran with years of service to the league, Commissioner Adam Silver was only weeks into the No. 1 job when the Sterling story broke. For anyone working in such a position of power, there will inevitably arrive what my Wharton colleague Professor Michael Useem calls a "leadership moment."[36] You don't often get a lot of warning before these moments arrive, and your actions when confronted by them are likely to become a large part of your legacy. As Useem has astutely written: "We all need to be ready for those moments when our leadership is on the line and the fate or fortune of others depends on what we do."[37]

When faced with his own leadership moment, Silver acted decisively—not to mention correctly in deed if not completely in words—in banning Sterling from the NBA for life and issuing the stiffest fine possible, $2.5 million.[38] I support Silver's actions—at the very least, the way he acted so very quickly and, after a level of diligence and due process, specifically noted "inclusion and respect" as the key factors lacking in the Sterling matter. But an even more impactful league leadership moment would have included one variation in rationale. I do not believe that this *single moment* of wrongdoing was adequate enough for the penalty extended. Silver noted that regarding this sanction, "we did not take into account his past behavior."[39] "Firing," as with Los Angeles Dodgers executive Al Campanis when he asserted that blacks lacked the "necessities" to manage in baseball and broadcaster Jimmy "the Greek" Snyder's claim that blacks had enough when asked about their absence as head coaches in the NFL, had been the long-standing response to racist commentary. However, that penalty here, based solely on Sterling's interaction with Stiviano, is somewhat questionable.[40] Sterling's fellow owner Mark Cuban of the Dallas Mavericks is among those who agree with me; after the penalties, he stated: "What Donald said was wrong. It was abhorrent. There's no place for racism in the NBA, any business I'm associated with. But at the same time, that's a decision I make. I think you've got to be very, very careful when you start making blanket statements about what people say and think, as opposed to what they do. It's a very, very slippery slope." He added: "How many people are bigoted in one way or the other in this league? I don't know. But you find one, all of a sudden you say, well, you can't play favorites being racist against African Americans. Where do you draw the line?"[41]

The line that Cuban expressed concern about, and a broader concern about the harsh penalty for speech, is well worth pondering. In the end, it was time for Sterling to go, but in my opinion the clarity is best stated by *his body of work* rather than his words to Stiviano alone, including his previous issues with charges of racism. For reasons one can only speculate upon, Adam Silver chose to focus on this most recent event as the sole reason for the lifetime ban and fine. Institutional messages have an impact. They serve as barometers of where we are as a society, and in some ways, institutional messages by sports entities are even more powerful; again, just look at the lasting impact on society of the integration of Major League Baseball by Jackie Robinson. The commissioner did indicate that further review would have incorporated an examination of the body of work. There was some belief that many owners did not want a hearing of any sort, for fear that their own racial and other negative skeletons might be rattled out. This became a reality when Atlanta Hawks owner Bruce Levenson announced that he would be selling his ownership interest because he had written an internal email with inappropriate racial themes.[42] Before a decisive hearing could take place, Steve Ballmer stepped in with essentially a preemptive offer to purchase the franchise.[43]

Who Makes the Games? The Athletes

Without visible acts like those of Sterling, too often the question raised to those who strive to point out nonexplicit racism is, "What are you complaining about?" But this blatant moment was different—so different that the protests of Sterling's actions were not met by bewilderment. The Sterling saga reminds me of Eduardo Bonilla-Silva's powerful work *Racism without Racists*. In it, the author describes the hesitancy that people of color have in accusing someone of acting in a racist manner, for fear of being accused of "playing the race card." The Sterling drama, however, was a rare moment where blacks could actually not be accused of playing the race card. After all, the TMZ tape was the smoking gun. Here is a particularly damaging exchange between Stiviano and Sterling, from the transcript later published by Deadspin:

> *Stiviano: Do you know you have a whole team that's black that plays for you?*
>
> *Sterling: You just, do I know? I support them and give them food, and clothes, and cars, and houses.*[44]

Racism and disrespect are rarely exposed so blatantly. It may have been this language that served as the key catalyst for action by the athlete segment of the Sports Power Matrix. This appeared to provide the athlete segment strength to act.

Sterling wasn't done there. As he continued his rant, he only went further in displaying a kind of racial arrogance that could truly be called reminiscent of an earlier era:

Sterling: . . . *Who gives it to them? Does someone else give it to them?* . . . *Who makes the game? Do I make the game, or do they make the game? Is there thirty owners, that created the league?*"[45]

In the NFL, during times of labor dispute the players' union has often used the rallying cry, "We are the game." Predictably, NFL owners have sometimes responded in a problematic way. Perhaps the most egregious—and controversial—of those responses came during the heated contract talks of 1987, when former union leader Gene Upshaw claimed that an NFL executive told him, "Players are like cattle and the owners are ranchers, and the owners can always get more cattle." They were powerful words, but after the NFL protested and produced documentation hinting that the language actually came from Upshaw himself, a judge ordered Upshaw's comment stricken from the record.[46] New National Basketball Players Association Executive Director Michele Roberts recently made a point about the relationship here: "Why don't we have the owners play half the games?" Roberts told *ESPN The Magazine.* "There would be no money if not for the players. Let's call it what it is. There. Would. Be. No. Money."[47] Sure, someone needs to organize the competition, but only a few can play these games at these extraordinary levels.

The Upshaw ruling notwithstanding, two things are clear about the athlete segment of the Sports Power Matrix—first, the players do have power; second, their power is used with much less frequency than that of the other segments, especially with regard to diversity and inclusion. There are a number of reasons for this, not the least of which is that the power that athletes possess is probably the most tenuous and fleeting of all of the parties involved. After all, most athlete careers are short. Athletes are also aware that there is always someone striving to take their job. They are replaceable.

In the Sterling case, however, the players *did* flex their muscles and did threaten to boycott the league if Sterling was allowed to stay, and this potential action was by all accounts real and impactful. It was an admirable and powerful act, one that could have only been made more powerful, in my opinion, if white players had been allowed to participate more fully. There was a strong threat that black players in the league would have refused to play for the Clippers if Sterling was allowed to continue as an owner; my presumption is that white players would have joined in as well. This, of course, would have made the action all the more powerful. This was a leadership moment for the players, and they seemed prepared to embrace it.

The Power of the Sponsors

Silver served as the visible conscience of the league. Promisingly, too, another segment did play a relatively powerful role in provoking rapid movement on the Sterling matter—the sponsors of the Los Angeles Clippers. Led most notably by State Farm Insurance and CarMax, sponsors who were financially tied to the Clippers made it clear they had no interest in being affiliated with the organization while this racial taint existed. They suspended their sponsorship contractual obligations, with great impact. CarMax, in their own corporate leadership moment, issued a stern and powerful statement: "These views directly conflict with CarMax's culture of respect for all individuals. While we have been a proud Clippers sponsor for nine years and support the team, fans and community, these statements necessitate that CarMax end its sponsorship."[48]

The franchise got the message. As the team's interim CEO, Richard Parsons, said: "If none of your sponsors want to sponsor you, coaches don't want to coach for you, players don't want to play for you, what have you got?"[49]

Beyond Race

Maybe the most amazing part of the coverage of the Sterling recording episode was how little mention was made of the sexist nature and tone of Sterling's interaction with Stiviano. This is in some ways surprising, given that I have often been advised by league and team officials that this sexism—the way male professional athletes treat women—has become perhaps the dominant respect issue in sports today. We will explore this issue further later in the book, but for all of the talk about the racial dynamics at play in the Sterling incident, there was little recognition that this was also an egregious moment of a lack of respect for women by one of the most powerful men in sport. This is an interesting insight into the composition of the entities that cover sport as well as who the decision makers are in newsrooms.

One further connecting event sheds light on the need for more vigilance through diversity and inclusion. The night Mark O'Mara joined me on CNN was just a few days after Cinco de Mayo. After our discussion about racism in sports, Lemon played a clip of MSNBC broadcasters pretending to celebrate the holiday with some poor stereotypes—shaking maracas, wearing sombreros, and making repeated references to getting drunk. It failed pretty severely as humor and drew the attention of many. A lesson was there for the taking: that a person of color was needed not at the top of the organization but in the editorial room, where the misguided decision was made to act out that scene. Only true inclusiveness in that MSNBC *big room*—and an accompanying diversity of ideas and sensitivities—could have prevented the firestorm that ensued. The complaints rolled in, and MSNBC, predictably, was forced to issue an apology.[50]

CHAPTER 2

Leadership and Inclusion
The NFL and the Ray Rice Affair

R ay Rice had been a stellar NFL running back for the Baltimore
Ravens for six seasons, and his story beyond the football field
was not especially unique. Even the disturbing allegation in February
2014 that he had physically abused his then-fiancée Janay Palmer
was, unfortunately, not an occurrence without precedent in society.
Sadly, the NFL and other major sports leagues had been struggling
with the issue of domestic violence for years.

This case was slightly more complicated, however, by the fact
that the celebrity gossip site TMZ had obtained and published a
video of the actual incident. The video showed, for all the world to
see, Rice dragging a visibly unconscious woman—Palmer—from an
elevator inside Atlantic City's Revel Casino.[51]

The public waited for months for the NFL to respond. For
how many games would Rice be suspended? How harshly would
he be punished? There was some degree of suspense over how the
league would treat a true "star player," but again, the story was
hardly a blockbuster. After initially being charged with third-degree
aggravated assault, Rice later had his charges dropped when he
agreed to undergo counseling. He and Palmer also got married. The
NFL, for its part, announced in July 2014—five months after the
TMZ tape was first published—that it had suspended Rice for . . .
two games of the 2014 season.[52]

That announcement was followed by a strong chorus in the
media, and especially on social media, that the punishment was not
harsh enough—that the league was soft on domestic abuse and that

35

it had missed an important opportunity to send a message about its stance on domestic violence. It was, all seemed to agree, a leadership moment missed, and broadly a grand moment where an entire segment of society, women, felt especially disrespected.

Facing criticism from all quarters, NFL commissioner Roger Goodell issued a statement on the matter, saying: "I take responsibility both for the decision and for ensuring that our actions in the future properly reflect our values. I didn't get it right. Simply put, we have to do better. And we will."[53] At the time, this seemed entirely reasonable—the idea that America's Game was going to listen to America. In the wake of the controversy, the league proudly announced new, stiffer sanctions for domestic violence. The crisis seemed to have been averted.

The Second Video

Of course, it wasn't. In fact, the crisis had only just begun.

The real problems emerged when TMZ released a second, much more dramatic video in September 2014. It may be unfair to judge Goodell as not understanding or even being properly advised on what domestic abuse actually looks like. After all, I too was jarred by the second TMZ video—a tape that showed the ferocity of the blow Rice delivered to Palmer.[54] Equally stunning was the apparent complete lack of concern Rice displayed in the immediate aftermath of the blow as he mindlessly moved her limp body from the elevator door and out into the hallway. Beyond the individual lack of respect, the lack of concern hadn't been seen in the previous tape, and the connection between the punch itself and the neglect that followed had to be viewed in succession in order to fully grasp the extent of the abuse.

If we could have imagined the blow before seeing that second tape, I'm guessing most of us could not have imagined his reaction. We wanted to see his regret—his horror at what he had done. In the 2001 movie *Baby Boy*, when the character Jody strikes his girlfriend Yvette, there is a sense of instant and visual regret.[55] Of remorse.

But this is, of course, mere fiction, and in some ways, it is a lie that we can allow ourselves to believe—a lie that we want to believe. Fortunately, for many of us, this or other Hollywood portrayals are the only experience we will ever have with domestic abuse. And I have to wonder: Is that fictionalized abuse the kind of offense that would have warranted a two-game suspension? Did we want to believe that Rice would have felt that immediate remorse that we see in the movies? In the end, should it have mattered? The second video displayed not only the punch, which may have been anticipated, but the apparent lack of remorse, which many of us thought would be there. But that lack-of-remorse analysis may be wrong, too. In a subsequent interview, Rice's wife explained that he reacted the way that he did because he was in shock.[56] This further amplifies the complexity of these matters and the need for those with real insight to be involved in responding.

Regardless of how we might answer, it was clear by the way society reacted to the tape that Americans expected the NFL—and Goodell—to take a stronger stand. After that second tape hit, women's groups, commentators, politicians, and others called for the commissioner to either resign or be fired. Media members, even those who had halfway defended Goodell for his earlier decision, turned against him. This was the fan and media segments of the Sports Power Matrix at work. Once, and arguably still, the most powerful man in sports, Goodell all at once found his career in peril. He ultimately survived. But according to many, the reason was more financial than moral: Goodell had helped his owners make millions during his tenure, and because he had done so, he had built up enormous goodwill.[57]

The Role of Due Process?

The criminal nature of Rice's actions in some ways made it more difficult for the NFL to act than if his offense in terms of "respect" had been more about, for instance, the use of offensive language as with Sterling. After all, in the United States, due process is the designated precursor to punishment, which is why even the existence of a video is not enough to result in conviction. The level of due process required in a criminal proceeding is generally a much higher standard than in a private setting, such as a sports league. Due process in a criminal proceeding, including the opportunity to present your case, is constitutionally protected. This contrasts starkly with the rapid penalties levied against Donald Sterling or the firings of Al Campanis and Jimmy the Greek. In each of those cases, private enterprises were able to act as swiftly as they desired, as the governmental standard of due process is not required. In each of those cases, too, although I applaud the speed, none of the leaders got it completely right, as Campanis and Snyder were too severely punished and Sterling was punished for the single event, not for his history of racism and disrespect.

So what of due process? Some in sports will speak about the need to let the wheels of justice turn and wait for the final outcome in the courts before having a player sit out or be suspended. The problem with that approach today, however, is this: with the explosion of social media, as public judges we often feel that, in lieu of the legal proceedings, we have the data we need to call for swift and powerful action. Little focus had been paid to this issue before now, but social media is increasingly putting the pressure on the sports world to get things "right" when it comes to punishing wrongdoing. There are the courts, and there are the rules of the league. But there is also the judge and jury that is social media—and it's an increasingly powerful court. In the end, the caution that leadership in sports should heed is that a person's livelihood should not be stripped absent due process. In a subsequent arbitration, it was ruled that Rice could not be punished more severely simply because a second video had appeared; that Rice had been truthful and forthcoming in the initial process, and that essentially a harsher punishment, due to the revelation of the second tape and presumably due to the public reaction, was improper.[58]

Due process, and leadership reacting to the public, is an issue across sports. At the collegiate level, two extremes in reaction time to breaking news can be seen in the way two Florida college football powerhouses, Florida and Florida State, handled the cases of quarterbacks Treon Harris and Jameis Winston, respectively. Harris, a redshirt freshman for the Gators, was immediately suspended by coach Will Muschamp following an accusation of sexual assault—an accusation, notably, that arrived on the same weekend of his breakout performance, one in which he helped his team to a comeback win over rival Tennessee. Two years earlier, by contrast, Winston was accused of an assault, and coach Jimbo Fisher did not suspend him. Under his leadership, the Florida State Seminoles went on to win the national championship, while Winston claimed the Heisman Trophy. He has since run afoul of the law and his school on other occasions; he was caught stealing crab legs from a grocery store and later was suspended for a game for using offensive language toward women in a university dining hall. He has faced no punishment at all for the assault accusation, even though Florida State officially launched an investigation into the matter in September 2014.[59]

Two years and no suspension at Florida State, versus suspension within 24 hours at the University of Florida. Does the role that sport plays in society demand that leadership move more swiftly than in the nonsports setting? And are swift, strong decisions any guarantee that those who make them will be rewarded by their constituencies? On that last question, I ask you to ponder this fact: as of this writing in December of the 2014–2015 college football season, Florida State was riding high in the polls and in the playoffs. Florida struggled mightily, and Muschamp has been fired. My view is that these athletes must be extended the same rights to participate and make a living as anyone else.

As would be the case with professionals in any field, we should let the legal system make its determination before a career is irreparably impacted.

Lessons Learned

The Rice case has brought several issues to the forefront. The actions of many of the young men who dominate in these sports are illustrative, in many instances, of a culture that most are fortunate to avoid—a culture where violence is such a common occurrence that it is impossible to avoid seeing or hearing it or its impact. But like anyone else, athletes deserve an appropriate level of due process, even in this private sector setting.

One broad lesson is the need for the various sports businesses to provide resources for individuals to avoid these types of events. The greater clarity needed is to find ways to ensure that athletes participate in these programs. Across leagues, encouraging players to participate in what are broadly called player development or player engagement programs is not always easy to do. Renewed efforts have taken place across leagues, particularly with regard to domestic violence. Wisely, too, the focus of the programming is not only on players but on league staffs and executives as well.

Beyond programming at the college and professional levels, we need to educate participants in youth and school sports about these issues at the earliest appropriate points in those programs. This would entail much work in making sure that coaches or others deliver the right instruction to both young athletes and their parents. These are sensitive issues, but framing them in terms of respect may be the correct course. Such programming could be an extension of the "No More" public service campaign featuring NFL players.[60] The public service announcements use celebrity to capture the attention of fans of all ages and drive them to an informational website. Sustained impactful programming could be provided via this website and offer age-appropriate curriculum with instruction on how best to deliver it.

An additional lesson, and one we also saw in the Sterling affair, is the poor decision making that occurred in the absence of both diversity and inclusion among key leadership regarding domestic violence. The actions following the public outcry after the second video was released revealed clearly an absence of expertise regarding domestic violence issues at the highest levels of the NFL. And no, this is not just about a lack of women in the executive suite; rather it's about a lack of understanding about how true diversity and true inclusion are key to delivering a culture of true respect. Absent diverse employees, consultants with the appropriate expertise may be the right strategy. The NFL did subsequently bring consultants on board.[61]

Though they were different kinds of incidents, it's notable that the Rice story occurred on the heels of both the Sterling controversy and the related one mentioned earlier that took place in Atlanta, in which Atlanta Hawks owner Bruce Levenson offered to relinquish his ownership interests in the team following the revelation of an email that contained negative racial commentary.[62] Then the football season got under way with the sobering news that All-Pro running back Adrian Peterson had beaten his four-year-old son with a switch. Here, there were photographs and texts to offer context for the story.[63] Peterson's team, the Minnesota Vikings, was notably impacted by the loss of a Radisson Hotels sponsorship when they reinstated the player.[64] The sponsor segment often moves without traditional due process. Their relationship is generally contractual, so they have the right to move as rapidly as they feel those agreements allow.

All of these incidents remind us of the new era in which we find ourselves—one where secrets are harder to keep, where uncovering racism is not dependent solely on the ignorance of the perpetrator, as was the case in the Campanis and Snyder moments in the 1980s, when both spewed racism with full knowledge of television cameras rolling.

We live in an era of sophistication. One of, as the book title states, *Racism without Racists*.[65] Absent membership in a white hate organization, expressions of old-school hatred are known to be problematic. But we have clearly not all caught on to the power of technology to capture what today's mind knows to keep private. Rice in an elevator. Sterling on tape. Levenson via email. Any number of players on Twitter. In a sense, this is the last frontier for the revelation of clandestine disrespectful beliefs, whether based on hate or simple ignorance. Those in all segments of the Sports Power Matrix are subject to the repercussions.

Without a doubt, however, and putting the realm of social media aside, the most important lesson in this matter is about domestic violence. From a leadership point of view, the takeaways are as follows: there is a need to act fast, while at the same time balancing swift action against a measured examination of the facts and due process, and any action will be best guided by the inclusion of a diverse set of viewpoints.

CHAPTER 3

Tone Deafness to Racism
The Washington Redskins and the Need for Respect and Equality

R *edskins.* Imagine the most offensive term ever used toward you, based on your race, ethnicity, gender, disability, or sexual orientation, or another aspect of your identity, and you'll probably arrive where I'm at in this debate about the name for this controversial National Football League franchise: The use of an offensive race-based name for an entity epitomizes disrespect. Which is to say this: there should be no debate at all. I'll refer to opinion polls and the like in this chapter, but in the end, no math should be allowed to be used in support of racism.

When we dream of a so-called postracial society, we collectively ask the same kinds of questions: When will we know that we are "there"? When will we experience that perfect moment of diversity, inclusion, respect, and equality, and no longer need to focus on these difficult issues? There are no answers to these questions, because as my flawed logic with diversity in ownership has taught me, there will not be just any single event that indicates we are "there." Rather especially in terms of equality, there will likely be *multiple* indicators that we are there. As with the arrival of black quarterbacks, little will probably be said about that moment once it arrives. There may be reflective, so-called "remember when" moments, but not much else.

However, I believe that one bit of progress that will be included in that new and better day is that there will no longer be a team called the Washington Redskins; we will see a permanent change in which a racist name is eliminated. The franchise has used the name since the year after it was founded as the Boston Braves, in 1932, and was certainly not alone in selecting a Native American–focused name. Other professional sports teams bear Native American nicknames even today, including the NFL's Kansas City Chiefs and baseball's Atlanta Braves and Cleveland Indians. But none are more controversial than the Redskins.[66]

The fact that this remains an issue—whether or not the word *Redskins* is racist—has always been puzzling to me. On the most basic level, I recall vividly watching television and movie westerns where the cowboys interchangeably called Native Americans "dirty savages" and "redskins." That's why it is a mystery to me why anyone would *not* recognize the negative nature of the phrase. Maybe you had to be a fan of the old westerns, and of a certain age, to truly have been immersed in the negative use of the word. But I'm not sure that's much of an excuse. The name is simply racist.

After all, for years now, the National Congress of American Indians, the oldest and largest American Indian organization representing about 150 tribes across the nation, has publicly stated that the term is "a racial slur."[67] I'm not sure what else I would need in order to take action if I owned a business with a name that many find offensive. But of course, other leaders in precisely that position in sports and other businesses have felt otherwise.

Leading the list are the proprietors of Sambo's Restaurant, who hold tightly to a derogatory name for a restaurant with an even more derogatory logo.[68] Around the globe any number of products have chosen only in recent decades to change their offensive names, including Darkie Toothpaste, a toothpaste sold by Colgate-Palmolive until 1989 featuring a logo that was a minstrel in blackface.[69] Numerous colleges and universities and even high schools, meanwhile, have discontinued the use of names referencing Native American tribes and peoples. Some entities, however, maintain a stubborn reluctance to relinquish the perceived value of a long-established brand.

Equality Defined, and Apparent Unconscious Racism

There is nothing special in this definition. If anything, this is the nonspecific catch-all principle—one that calls for fair treatment of all parties, by all parties, particularly where they are similarly situated. No one should be treated differently because of who they are. As has been discussed throughout this book, where someone is treated differently due to his or her "difference," or not included for that same reason, that constitutes an inequality. Similarly, inequality of treatment may be found where no "traditional" difference is involved. This will be discussed more extensively with regard to the Miami Dolphins bullying incident.

The arguments to continue the use of the name range from strained justifications based on tradition to plain old economics. Notably and perhaps sadly, however, the continued use of these names is also supported by public opinion polls approving of the use of the name by both Americans broadly and Native Americans specifically.[70]

A 2014 Associated Press–GfK poll, for instance, showed that Americans supported the use of the Redskins name.[71] Seventy-nine percent, or essentially four in five Americans, indicated in the survey that they do not think the team should change its name. Only 11 percent thought the name should be changed, while 8 percent were not sure and 2 percent did not answer. Only 18 percent of nonwhites felt that the name should change. The nearly 80 percent who favored keeping the name represented a 10 percent drop from the last national poll on the subject, conducted in 1992 by the *Washington Post* and *ABC News* just before the team won its last Super Bowl. At that time, 89 percent said the name should not be changed, and 7 percent said it should.[72]

Another poll used regularly by supporters of the name is conducted by the Annenberg Public Policy Center at the University of Pennsylvania.[73] That poll, conducted in 2004, polled 768 Native Americans about the use of the Redskins name and found that only 9 percent found the name offensive. According to the Redskins franchise and others who support it, of course, this poll has been used as evidence that, since Native Americans don't find the name offensive, nobody else should either. Polling science aside, however, I join the chorus of those who have asked, "How reliable is a poll of only 768 people?"

Of course, even as these polls have indicated that the public at large may be okay with the use of this name, many others—including stakeholders within the Native American community—have forcibly fought back. Former US Senator Ben Nighthorse Campbell of Colorado, who is Native American, has said that the term *Redskins* is especially damaging because of its origins and its use in connection with bounties on Indians. "There's a derogatory name for every ethnic group in America, and we shouldn't be using those words," he said. "We probably haven't gotten our message out as well as it should be gotten out."[74] Countless other activists have joined his cause in recent years as well.

The ongoing debate, which seems to grow more heated with each passing season, has featured lawsuits, the purchase of airtime by tribes arguing against the name, politicians including President Barack Obama chiming in, and public relations messages from the team itself.[75] Certain media outlets have gone so far as to refuse to use the name in their reporting.[76] And yet the owners have been allowed to do what they desire with their name. That decision has been to continue on as the Redskins.

Much like Adam Silver's leadership moment in the Donald Sterling matter, there is a need for somebody in a position of power to act here. Washington's leadership has said they will not change, and the non-ownership segments either have shown a lack of desire or simply don't have enough power to enact change. When it comes to the latter, Native Americans must certainly be included in that group.

The Athletes

In the midst of this debate, some have asked why players have chosen not to act. This is an interesting situation to ponder. First, no matter how blatant the racism here—and the need to act—may seem to some, the issue is complex, especially for players. I have interviewed a number of former Redskins players and they have all told me that it was not an issue they contemplated in their time there. Many of them told me, not surprisingly, that their biggest concern was protecting their job; part of that often requires them to draw as little attention to themselves as possible. A recent poll showed that 58 percent of NFL players believed the name should be retained.[77]

Unlike the Sterling situation, there is no threat of a player boycott in the Redskins case, because in the Sterling case, players were *directly impacted* by Sterling's actions. There Sterling was disrespecting African Americans. He did not want black people at his games. That's not the case in Washington. That franchise is not peopled by Native Americans. Yes, players could take action here if they had the political will, but they also have the most to lose. Given the players' relative lack of political will, then, the most obvious leader and potential change agent here would be the team's owner, Dan Snyder. But instead of facing the reality that the time has come for change, Snyder and his franchise have taken an adamant stance against any change. In fact, he once told a reporter from *USA Today,* defiantly: "We'll never change the name. It's that simple. NEVER. You can use caps."[78] This stance is sadly reflective of the insulation and power that sports franchise owners possess, and also of a lack of diversity and inclusion among his leadership team. This insulation allows an individual to be nonresponsive and disrespectful to the views of even a minority of individuals, to be nonresponsive to their passion and the direct impact that a stance has on them.

The fact that Snyder has engaged in the public conversation at least indicates an awareness of the issue. But when people attack a brand, that brand owner must pay attention. It is in his financial interest.

This is not to say that Snyder is being insincere, however. There is what I would term an "alma mater-esque tone" in his responses. This tone is echoed by many and can be read in Washington newspapers almost daily. But honest or not, it shows a deafness to the racism inherent in the name—and that deafness is hardly limited to Snyder alone. I have stopped being amazed, for example, at how many Washington, DC–based African Americans love their franchise and cherish the name. It would seem that African Americans of all groups would appreciate the powerlessness of Native Americans on this issue and the negative nature of the name.[79]

Ownership's Refusal to Act

In his 2013 letter to fans on this issue, Snyder wrote: "I respect the feelings of those who are offended by the team name. But I hope such individuals also try to respect what the name means, not only for all of us in the extended Washington Redskins family, but among Native Americans too."[80] In this instance, Snyder alludes to the argument that the association with the team "honors" Native Americans. This is where we have to pause to reflect on leadership as well as courage. One can certainly argue that Snyder is leading, and that he is leading for what he indicates he believes in. One might even argue that there is a display of courage as well. In the sense that he is a true believer, it certainly takes courage to stand by those beliefs in this moment.

Management and Ownership: Insensitivity or Lack of Inclusion?

The insular nature of those who are included in Snyder's personal circle of power is reflected in a letter that was written by Bruce Allen, the president of the Washington Redskins, in response to Senator Harry Reid and fifty other United States senators who had written to the team relaying their belief that the time for the name change had come. Allen reiterated much of what Snyder had written the previous year, reflecting on the involvement of his father, former Redskins head coach George Allen, in the creation of the current logo in 1971 and noting that the logo was created in conjunction with Native American leaders.

But Allen also focuses on the term as an "expression of solidarity." "More than a decade ago one of the foremost scholars of Native American languages, Smithsonian Institution senior linguist Ives Goddard, spent seven months researching the subject and concluded that the word 'redskin' originated as a Native American expression of solidarity by multi-tribal delegations that traveled to Washington to negotiate Native American national policies."[81]

"There is nothing that we feel is offensive," Allen added. "And we're proud of our history."[82]

Here is my question, however. When we reflect on respect and equality in our culture, are the feelings of those in power really the key concern? Do we care how that segment "feels"? Even NFL commissioner Roger Goodell has provided support for the continuation of the Redskins name. In a letter addressed to ten members of Congress who wrote to him for support, he noted that the name "from its origin represented a positive meaning distinct from any disparagement that could be viewed in some other context" and that the name was never "meant to denigrate Native Americans or offend any group."[83]

The Political Segment: Notable Efforts in a Leadership Vacuum

US representative Betty McCollum, who has joined with her fellow members of Congress in saying the time for change has come, asked and answered the following question: "Would Roger Goodell and Dan Snyder actually travel to a Native American community and greet a group of tribal leaders by saying, 'Hey, what's up, redskin?' I think not. . . . Indian children, families and elders are Americans, and just like all racial, ethnic or religious groups, they deserve to be treated with respect and dignity, not as a demeaning caricature or mascot. That shouldn't be too much to ask of the NFL."[84] McCollum, to the extent that she can, has tried to push for change. Among those in the external segments beyond those including owners, managers, and players, she's not alone.

The "proud origins" defense can only go so far, as can the "alma-mater-esque" stance I mentioned earlier. After all, we've seen impressive leadership on this issue at the lower levels of football—both in college and in high school. Schools individually as well as under the leadership of late NCAA president Myles Brand moved away from the use of Native American mascots and names in just over the past two decades. Among the institutions that have dropped offensive names are St. John's University (from the Redmen to the Red Storm), Marquette University (from Warriors to Golden Eagles), and Stanford University, which switched in the early 1970s from the Indians and eventually became the Cardinal. Syracuse University, Miami University in Ohio, and others have also changed their names.[85]

Name changing is not new to sports or even the Washington, DC, area. The Washington Wizards of the NBA were once the Washington Bullets. But because of violence in DC and elsewhere, then-owner Abe Pollin took the leadership step to change the name.[86] No doubt the name did not have the brand value of the Redskins, but the change was made and, by all accounts, the franchise survived just fine.

Some colleges and schools have continued to use Native American names, with some doing so even as activists have encouraged them to drop them. In other words, the Redskins are not alone in their stubbornness; they aren't even the only sports team in the country that use the term *redskin*.[87]

The Economics of Change

There is a financial angle to this entire debate. The US Patent and Trademark Office recently ruled that the Redskins trademark was not protected, and that powerful ruling probably prompted a deeper economic review by owners and managers. That ruling, however, is being appealed.[88]

More broadly, some have discussed the potential costs of changing a franchise name—whether the Redskins or some other franchise. I give this issue little shrift. A key reason is the enormous revenues shared each year among NFL franchises—each team pulls in $150 million annually based on television revenue alone.[89] In other words, even if there were some negative impact on merchandise sales or other fan support of the franchise, which I doubt, it would be nominal relative to the other revenues.

The major expense to the franchise would be the creation of a new name and logo and the replacement of items such as stationery, uniforms, signage, and other messaging. One estimate has placed this cost at around $5 million, and the former Charlotte Bobcats of the NBA estimated that their transition back to the Hornets would cost them about $4 million. Again, this is a nominal amount for a franchise that is worth about $2 billion, with annual revenues approaching $375 million.[90] The Hornets have also noted record sales of Hornets gear in addition to a renewed level of interest in the franchise.[91]

Protests, legal actions, and threatened legal actions are not unique in bringing about greater diversity. For example, when the then Cleveland Rams moved to Los Angeles in the 1940s, the team's use of the Los Angeles Memorial Coliseum was made contingent upon its agreement to sign black players. All of this evidence, in other words, points to a simple truth: External segments can have an impact in this area as well.[92]

The Sponsors

Contrary to sponsors playing a major positive role in acting on Donald Sterling when his behavior was wrong, no sponsors stepped up with regard to the Redskins. Federal Express is the naming rights sponsor of the stadium where the Redskins play, FedEx Field. The connection between that corporate entity and the Redskins is much more significant, financially and visibility-wise, than is the sponsor arrangement between CarMax or State Farm and the Clippers.

Members of the Oneida nation formally sought a shareholder vote to reconsider the $205 million naming rights deal.[93] They received only 0.1 percent of the shareholder votes cast, with 99.9 percent supporting the FedEx Field relationship with the Redskins. That is a vivid example of the absence of both political and economic power and the consequences of not having either.[94]

Wielding Ownership and Management Power: Doing the Right Thing

With the polls and even if a majority of Native Americans and Federal Express shareholders are fine with the use of the name, there is a need to act. Why disrespect even a small segment of society, especially when alternatives exist? This takes us into the perception of disrespect too. Even if the Redskins leadership truly believe they are correct, should they not be sensitive to what someone perceives as the respect they deserve, particularly if this perception is reasonable? In some ways this chapter has raised the important distinction between diversity and inclusion. Diversity in most societal settings has become easier to attain as we've become a more diverse society. In sports, diversity on the field of play is relatively easy. But the key, illustrated here regarding decision making on important issues of respect, is inclusion in the power decision-making processes. Sometimes a more diverse set of viewpoints must be sought in order to make the most inclusive decisions. Even the most diverse businesses are not diverse in every possible way.

With the Redskins, change will not come as easily. That's because, as much as I personally don't see it, the Redskins name change remains hotly debated—and many remain who see no problem with the name at all. The advocates for change are not having an impact in Snyder's *big room*. That's why, again, the segments of the Sports Power Matrix must take it upon themselves to act. Sometimes it takes a societal sea shift before a leader decides the time to change is right, even if it differs from his or her personal preferences. This is particularly the case when the respect issue in question impacts one of the most powerless groups in America.

CHAPTER 4

Beyond Bullying
What the Miami Dolphins Matter Tells Us about Respect in the Workplace and Beyond

In November 2013, news broke that a Miami Dolphins player named Jonathan Martin had left the team.[95] He did not leave because of a contract dispute. He did not leave because of injury. Rather, he left, he said, because he was being bullied. This may be the most complex of the illustrations I use in this book. I, and many others, are still not sure exactly why what happened in this locker room occurred, but the public report provides a framework for this issue and the nuance of how we treat and respect one another. This was a dispute between two ballplayers that saw the light of day. Had this been two men of the same race, this book might be lacking a chapter, because the situation would not have been elevated to the level it reached.

The idea and definition of bullying is complex even in the context of a schoolyard, but the Martin case made clear to the entire nation that nobody is immune from bullying—not even a 312-pound Stanford-educated black man playing professional football. Society often creates stereotypes for bullying victims—outcasts in the halls of high schools, for instance, or members of the lesbian, gay, bisexual, transgender, and queer (LGBTQ) community—but here the victim was the towering Martin, an elite, powerful, and accomplished athlete who was nonetheless found by an investigator to have been tortuously bullied by three teammates, including a man who claimed to be a friend, Richie Incognito. The victimization included verbal taunts against Martin personally and insulting and degrading language directed toward his family members.[96]

When the facts were in, it seemed that Martin was targeted by his teammates for the simple reason that he was "different." In many ways this was locker room culture in the extreme. But as I noted, it was elevated and displayed for the public to scrutinize. Martin was a classics major at Stanford and a middle-class African American whose parents attended Harvard. He went to a private high school in Los Angeles. There is no such thing as a typical NFL player, but Martin certainly was unique in many aspects. For many, Martin's victimization opened a window into how bullying is connected more directly with "difference" than any specific personality or physical trait. Wrongly, we expect our athletes—male athletes, especially— to be overly muscled and immune to abuse. We may also unfairly expect that because of their size and strength, they are inherently less intelligent than the average person who is cursed with more brain than brawn. But guys who are different appear in the locker room every day. This scenario provides a bit of insight on the need to respect some in the way they feel they need to be respected.

This case provides an example of the nuance of respect in ways that we may not typically think about, and beyond the traditional categories often contemplated in discussions of diversity and inclusion.

Respect Defined: Beyond Mere Tolerance

As I wrote at the outset of this book, of all of the ideas I explore here, respect may well be the most complex. With diversity and inclusion, the clear focus is on the continued vigilance needed to accomplish certain goals; in some ways it's about numbers. Regarding respect, however, the definition in this space is one of *levels*. For example, simple "tolerance," for many, is enough—that is, letting people who are different exist without interference. No matter Sterling's view of blacks, he tolerated them. Respect, however, is a bit more challenging. In fact, I view respect as the next step in the continuum *beyond* tolerance.

This is a continuum that can, and should with time, advance society to a greater acceptance than we see today. But the beginning of that continuum, where we stand today, should also include the acknowledgment, if only internally, that individuals have rights and privileges, and that their differences are simply part of the society in which we live. Respect places an affirmative obligation to act positively, far beyond a "tolerance" to allow someone to exist.

Full *acceptance* is a desirable goal, and an understanding of respect can help parties move in that direction, but full acceptance also requires a great deal more mental gymnastics. For the racist, the homophobic, and the anti-Semitic, acceptance is where the most difficult transitions come.

Disrespectful Language as Everyday Language

After the Dolphins matter came to light, attorney Ted Wells of Paul, Weiss, Rifkind, Wharton & Garrison conducted and published an investigation on behalf of the NFL.[97] Though by no means the primary focus of the report, one standout finding was the use by Dolphins players of the word *nigger*—specifically, the casual use of the word in this interracial setting. Putting aside the common usage of the word in the streets, music, and film, the Dolphins case provided an example of how the word is used frequently in real, day-to-day life. It was in some ways shocking, and the Wells Report therefore only stoked further an ongoing societal discussion about the word and its usage; indeed, as early as the 1960s comedian-activist Dick Gregory wrote a book titled *Nigger* in efforts to take the sting out of a word with such a negative history.

Nigger was hardly the only slur covered by Wells, however. His report also highlighted how slurs against people who are Asian or LGBTQ had become a part of the regular banter among the players in Miami. Illustrative of the extent of this particular workplace problem was the utterly distressing catalog of language regularly used in that locker room: *nigga, dirty Pakistani, darkness, Chinaman, faggot, cunt, pussy,* and *Jap.* Predictably, there was even more disrespectful language toward women. As the Wells Report noted: "We did not approach this assignment expecting to discover behavior that society might anticipate in, say, an accounting firm or a law office. For better or worse, profanity is an accepted fact of life in competitive sports, and professional athletes commonly indulge in conduct inappropriate in other social settings. We also recognize that good-spirited goading often contributes to team bonding. But limits should exist."[98]

But what kind of limits? And what lessons can society really learn from the sports business workplace—or more specifically from a football locker room? Well, the answer is this: It is a unique venue but more ordinary than one might think. Over the past two years a series of events, some related, some not, have made sports the focus of debate regarding workplace issues such as offensive language and respect of an individual's sexual identity. And in these events—how they unfolded and how they were handled—we can gain insights into how different segments of the Sports Power Matrix can leverage their unique power to create a more "respectful" culture.

A Difficult Challenge

John Wooten is the chairman of the Fritz Pollard Alliance. That organization was formed on March 10, 2003, with the mission of promoting equality in job opportunities in coaching, front offices, and scouting in the NFL. Wooten was a player in the NFL from 1959 to 1968 for the Cleveland Browns and the Washington Redskins, and he has worked in other capacities for the league for decades. In his current role, he has also become the loudest voice against the use of the word *nigger* in the NFL workplace. "There is no place for it in our game" is a refrain I have heard from many other NFL insiders regarding the use of what polite society has come to refer to as "the n-word." Wooten falls squarely in that camp. As he says: "We want this word to be policed from the parking lot to the equipment room to the locker room . . . we want it eliminated completely and want it policed everywhere."[99]

Wooten and others in the NFL are caught in a bit of a generational bind. The word that was, and remains to many, the most derogatory term in existence in reference to African Americans has found a fraternal space in conversation in popular culture. In some sense, the word *nigger* has become what the Washington Redskins organization argues regarding their controversial name—an "acceptable" term. Wooten, one of the smartest, sagest men in football, knows this. Such is part of the battle he has decided to wage.

Some claim that acceptable usage of that word is a matter of context, or even pronunciation (*nigga* vs. *nigger*). This conversation has caused me to review my usage of the word in both casual and what have come to be known as "clinical" settings—in the classroom, in writing, and otherwise. I am in transition in my thinking as I write. Although I use the phrasing "the n-word" on occasion, I find it disingenuous and every bit as negative as the actual word. At the same time, I don't like the idea of giving others "permission" to use the word by virtue of my using it, even in a clinical fashion. So I find myself falling short of a total personal prohibition of use, even as I understand how impactful that full transition by me and others could be.

The irony of the Dolphins case and the Redskins discussion and the action being taken and not taken in Washington versus the concern about the word *nigger* is more than intriguing. Both terms are problematic, and both have constituencies arguing against their negativity. There is a key distinction: *nigger* is used in popular culture in a variety of ways, whereas *redskin*, other than as the name of athletic teams, exists solely as a derogatory word.

But back to our discussion of power. The power in this workplace issue—not only with regard to bullying, but also racism, sexism, and general intolerance of "difference"—touches the entire Sports Power Matrix.

Player behavior, in the athlete segment, captures so much of our attention and has such a powerful impact on our society; there is a long debate over whether athletes are role models, but we can all agree that what they do, especially if it is bad behavior, makes the news. That is precisely the case in what is, in its barest form, a dispute between two ballplayers.

In a broad sense, in settings where there is a real problem, the Sports Power Matrix is a good overlay to use to think about addressing these issues. Owners and managers have an important role to play here, with their efforts to craft a truly respectful workplace, as do sponsors, who have the power to choose whether to work with an organization based on their workplace environment. Similarly, fans can have an impact by not attending the games of a given team or league when serious issues—domestic violence, bullying, racism, sexism, and so on—come to light. Media also plays a key role—for example, in choosing to use or not use the Redskins name.

Ending the use of offensive language in day-to-day conversation is uniquely difficult. In part, that's because banning any type of language, offensive or not, is problematic. The NFL has found itself facing both praise and criticism for reportedly engaging in conversations about rules banning the use of the word *nigger* during games.[100] But when this type of activity occurs, or when it is known to occur regularly, what can those in the ownership and management segments do to change a culture that finds little problem with the language in question?

Positive Action: How the Stakeholders Must Respond

The Dolphins had in place a workplace conduct policy that was taken straight from the NFL handbook:

Harassment can include, but is not limited to: unwelcome contact; jokes, comments and antics; generalizations and put-downs; pornographic or suggestive literature and language. In addition, harassment and discrimination are not limited to the workplace; they example [sic], through calls, texts, or emails, on a plane or team bus; at a team event; or at the team hotel.[101]

The policy was on the books. And that was of course important. But the real key for the Dolphins was to act—to seize the leadership moment—once the issues surfaced. Of course, many observers wanted more than the shipping off of the two players primarily involved, including the firing of top management personnel for allowing this culture to develop in the first place. The team asked the league to conduct an independent investigation. The league responded by retaining Wells. And then team owner and chairman Steve Ross issued a statement amplifying the leadership message:

The NFL locker room is a special place, no doubt, but that does not mean that different rules of decency and respect should be in play. Winning championships is what we are all about, but we cannot do so if any of our family members are challenged from reaching their potential.[102]

The Wells Report noted that Ross went further in stating, "There will not be any racial slurs, or harassing, or bullying in [the Dolphins] workplace, in that locker room and outside the locker room."[103]

So the tone was set at the top. But what of the players?

Although not highlighted in the report, one of the difficult issues the Dolphins brought up was the same issue Gregory identified years ago and the same issue that continues in popular culture today—the regular use of the word *nigger* by African Americans in interactions ranging from casual to the most public of settings. It is striking how this evolution has occurred, and equally striking how much conflict there is about what the "right" path forward is. A subtext in the conversation is whether blacks alone have the right to use the word, and the NFL offers context for that debate, too. In the lead-up to the 2013 season, Philadelphia Eagles wide receiver Riley Cooper, a white man, was caught on tape using the word while attending a concert. His case, and the Eagles' handling of it, lingered in the news for weeks, and it continues to hang over Cooper today. Issues were elevated in the Dolphins incident, I contend, because one player was white and one was black. Had this involved two black players in the key role, this may have been much less of a story.

Gregory's work, along with that of comedians such as Richard Pryor, has had a great influence over a generation of people of many ethnicities who have come to accept that the word can be used in certain situations. I look to an earlier generation—mine, specifically—as having guilt in this for broad usage of the word, even if only among ourselves. One reason the Gregory moment was so shocking for us was that the unwritten rule was not to use the word in front of whites. Thus, the confusion on the part of some whites, if not our culture as a whole, as to whether there is now a pass or permission to use, as with the word *redskin*, the most derogatory word for a race. In other words, yes, cultural barriers within sports are impeding progress on issues related to language and respect. But that progress must remain a goal, because what sport does in this space can clearly have a societal impact.

This is another opportunity for sport to guide young children about this potentially explosive language and the history of hate associated with many of these words. This is not likely to be direct guidance—in other words, from player or owner to youth—but rather guidance by virtue of actions taken and image presented. This, of course, is not the obligation of sport alone, but a place where youth sports programs can have a powerful and lasting impact.

Illustrative for youth, for example, would be the history of the origins of the word *nigger* (or other hate words, for that matter).

In the continuum of more openness and wider use of the word, explanations about the early usage by white slave masters wielding power over slaves would be educational for those who are not fully aware, as would be insights on the derogatory use of *nigger* in a power-executing manner in more recent times. The goal of such activities would be to give those who use the word, especially against oneself, complete information. This is what sport should do in this regard. All of the segments of the Sports Power Matrix have the ability to impact this space by exercising their unique powers.

Gay Men in the Locker Room

As the Dolphins case was occurring, so, too, were new issues regarding the presence of gay athletes in sports and in the locker room—or perhaps more specifically, the male locker room. Stories began to swirl and leagues began to discuss—either openly or privately—their plans for the day when gay men were open about their sexual orientation while playing major American sport. The issue percolated for a while and finally became "the" story in sports when Michael Sam, a defensive end at the University of Missouri, was drafted in the last round of the 2014 NFL draft by the St. Louis Rams. When that pick was announced, he became the first openly gay man to be drafted into the NFL. Sam's story, which is still unfolding, takes us deeper into issues of tolerance and respect in the sports world, though what this "moment" tells us is still unclear; as of this writing, Sam had been released first by the Rams and later by the Dallas Cowboys and was looking for a new team as a free agent. As *The Advocate* wrote upon his release from the Cowboys: "There are a lot of reasons why Sam's self-outing matters, and they have been said before. He is a pioneer. He is standing up to ignorant people who don't think a gay man can be a macho, tough football player. He is risking his personal success and possibly his career to come out prior to being drafted. He is changing the tides."[104]

I did not see this as the second coming of a Jackie Robinson moment. I do believe that such barrier breaking is significant and worthy of appropriate celebration, but the elements and magnitude of the Jackie Robinson moment remain unsurpassed. And to make the point again, a single barrier broken generally represents change, not progress.

In women's sports, of course, Billie Jean King and Martina Navratilova led the way in tennis decades before the issue was broadly discussed in "male" sports, so when Brittney Griner came out as gay as she entered the WNBA from Baylor University, there was barely a shrug in the sports world or in the media. In a bit of a twist from the overly macho expectations of the male athlete, for females one could argue that there is a societal expectation of a *lack* of femininity, as that characterization is traditionally defined according to gender stereotypes. Thus the fact that a female athlete is gay receives a relatively humdrum reaction in popular culture. That is more of what progress looks like, but again, that's on the field of play. An example of progress, for example, is Billie Jean King's World Team Tennis, a sports league that she founded in the 1970s and continues to lead today.[105]

But even on the women's side, much complex remains to be achieved. A decade ago at Penn State, a failure of leadership was brought to light in a lawsuit that alleged that a coach was discriminating against athletes who were lesbian or who did not act and dress in what she considered to be an appropriately heterosexual way. The matter came to light as lawsuits were filed after the dismissal of players from her team. These allegations occurred before the more famous matter involving the child abuse case with coach Jerry Sandusky, but is of major importance as well. It is illustrative of the power leadership can have to either provide or hinder equal opportunities for all, including lesbian and bisexual women athletes.[106] Clearly there is a need to remain vigilant, even where many believe progress has been achieved. This lawsuit was ultimately settled out of court.

The NBA had a similarly big story, a little more than a year before the Sam story hit. There, NBA veteran Jason Collins announced that he was gay. He was later signed by the Brooklyn Nets and officially became the first openly gay player to play in the NBA. The societal question that was asked at the time focused not so much on Collins but rather on how the other players in the locker room would react to a gay player being there. Before Collins came the announcement by soccer player Robbie Rogers.[107]

On the men's side, the entry of Sam and Collins certainly represents change. On our scale of progress on the field of play, there is clearly a great distance to go. The ongoing problems surrounding women and gender are indicative of how challenging true progress will be at this level. Absent blatant homophobia, just as with racism, discrimination will be hard to detect and directly address.

Thus far, at least in public reports, the change in the male locker room is occurring in a respectful fashion with few incidents.[108] This is clearly an instance where vigilance will be required for progress to truly take place. This is a step on the change continuum, but again, change on the field of play is so much less important in terms of progress than change in the true power positions. In sports, Rick Welts as the openly gay president of the Golden State Warriors, and in the corporate world, Tim Cook, the openly gay CEO of Apple, is the type of change we seek.[109]

The Real Goal: Achieving Broader Societal Impact

These issues are complex both in and out of sports and continue to be a work in progress for our society. There is a growing recognition of the impact that sports leagues, owners, and players can have beyond sport. The optics of greater respect within sports can create greater tolerance and civility in other societal sectors as well.

Sports should be trying to find ways to positively impact youth on these issues: to encourage them to make the right decisions, to teach them not to bully. I prefer the goal of teaching all to be respectful.

This imagery is different from saying, "Don't bully," particularly when there is a bit of a burden to understand what it takes for an individual to feel respected. We must instill in youth the idea that they should respect differences and that they must clearly understand the history of the word *nigger* and other slurs regarding race and gender identity. But these important goals can be achieved only if sports takes proactive, positive steps to create a more respectful culture.

In sports and in society, leadership requires quick and decisive action. The Silver model in many respects leads the way in these matters. Once information is vetted, swift, decisive action should take place. However, such action must include due process for the parties involved: athlete, owner, or whoever. The actions of both Silver in the Sterling case and Ross in the Dolphins case make clear the need for substantial follow-up as well. They also show that, as in any setting, leadership moves will not always be roundly applauded and will be viewed by many to fall short.

But proclaiming an act "wrong" or even punishing the culprit is not *all* that can be done. Resources should be committed to fully addressing issues of respect in the workplace itself as well as among those who will one day be a part of it. These actions can and must be led by the ownership segment—after all, they hold the greatest power—but as we have discussed here, when it comes to issues as dramatic as those seen in Los Angeles and Miami, all segments have an obligation to do their part as well.

CHAPTER 5

Respecting the Athlete
Compensation, Equality, and Complex Dynamics in "Amateur" Sports

S tunning as she is in her presence and athletic skill, at this point we have no idea whether the legend that is Mo'ne Davis will be with us much beyond the 2014 Little League World Series. Girls had played in the Little League World Series before, but this 13-year-old became a national sensation after helping her underdog team from Philadelphia advance all the way to the semifinals. With intense media scrutiny all around her, and with the entire nation watching, she deflected the attention to the other members of her team. All of them boys.[110]

Little League baseball is not just about kids playing a game in parks across the country. The enterprise is reported to have $85 million in assets and recently signed a television deal worth $76 million. The CEO, Steve Keener, makes a salary of $430,844.[111] In other words, it may not be a $10 billion behemoth like the NFL, but it's also not a nonprofit enterprise as amateurism advocates might fancy—a sport for the glory of sport alone.

A former pro athlete sent me a text as he prepared to drive his own young teenage daughter out to Williamsport, Pennsylvania, to watch Davis pitch in what turned out to be a losing effort against Las Vegas. He wrote: "Driving my daughter to Williamsport this morning to watch Mo'ne Davis pitch in the Little League World Series. Thought about you as I wondered about the loss of revenue

opportunities for her and her family. No one in the 75-year history
of this event has had the impact that she has. All of the gear/hats
are sold out. She's on the cover of *Sports Illustrated*/Good Morning
America . . . it's crazy. Someone should do an analysis. . . ."

In this sense, Davis is much closer to the reality of "amateurism"
that got college sports into the situation it confronts today. At this
most basic level, much like Magic Johnson being an exemplary black
man that no one should hate from a philanthropic perspective, who
could want this teenage girl, who is doing all of the right things, to be
treated unfairly? Should she really be burdened in the eighth grade
with worries about how any actions she takes now might ruin her
college athletic opportunities? The answer is no. But sadly, that's the
reality in which she finds herself. Every step of the way, because of
the "amateurism" rules of the NCAA, Davis needed to be on her toes.
The NCAA rules prohibit a myriad of behaviors, including receiving
anything of value based on your athletic ability. And indeed, the
University of Connecticut received a reprimand from the NCAA
for a recruiting violation regarding Davis. UConn's offense? Its head
basketball coach, Geno Auriemma, called Davis to congratulate
her on a job well done. The NCAA did, however, provide a unique
ruling allowing Davis to participate in a commercial aired during
the World Series and to receive compensation for that as well. This
was the right decision by the NCAA.[112] The NCAA recognized the
breadth of the moment too, noting the historic limits for this type of
participation for girls and women in sport.[113]

Amateurism?

I always hesitate a bit in using the word *amateur*. We all have
different visions of what that word references. Those images range
from ancient Greeks frolicking in fig leaves while playing various
sports to college athletes being cheered on by fraternity men wearing
raccoon-skin coats. Whatever your imagery may be, however, the

oldest vestiges of what constitutes an amateur athlete are outdated. And the ancient version we had almost universally come to accept as some glorious past never even existed. As classicist David C. Young writes in his book *The Olympic Myth of Greek Amateur Athletics*, we "can find no mention of amateurism in Greek sources, no reference to amateur athletes—no evidence that the concept 'amateurism' was even known in antiquity. The truth is that 'amateur' is one thing for which the ancient Greeks never even had a word."[114] He notes further that there were competitions where athletes could win prizes valued at ten years' worth of wages.[115] But some still envision the college athletes of today as living some kind of ancient ideal—playing the game for the pure love of the sport.

And in some ways, they are. The NCAA and the other governing bodies of college sport are among the last remaining entities in the world limiting participation to those who engage in sport for the glory of sport alone. In the best of circumstances, these athletes participate in exchange for an all-expenses-paid college education. Some don't even receive that. In stark contrast, over the last few decades, the Olympic world has loosened the reins on amateurism and allowed revenues to flow to athletes. The Olympics have survived.

Equality and Amateurism

But what is the "equality" question here? Where is the power? It is not *all* about money, but that is what will dominate the discussion in this chapter—more specifically the distribution and use of funds. Absent ownership, the power segments in this amateur world are the same as the pro world discussed earlier. Management here is the athletic administrators, including the NCAA or Little League leadership. The players here are student-athletes.

The revenues that are flowing to management and not to student-athletes have gotten the attention of many. There is a particular concern that the primary generators of those revenues, football and men's basketball, are not receiving them, and further, that those who play any of the other sports are "free-riding" on the revenues generated by these select athletes. The huge television contracts for the broadcast of the NCAA basketball tournament, the salaries of coaches such as Alabama's Nick Saban, and the rights fees received by the major conferences have not gone unnoticed. We're talking hundreds of millions of dollars. If recently passed NCAA rules continue to survive internal organizational scrutiny, the largest sports conferences may have even greater flexibility in how they distribute these greater revenues, even to student-athletes. The rule change of the NCAA Division I board primarily affects the 65 schools in the Atlantic Coast, Big Ten, Big 12, Pacific-12, and Southeastern conferences—collectively known as the Power 5.[116] So change is coming, and that change may benefit the athletes. The question is how much—and whether that will be enough.

Reassessing Amateurism

All of those concerned with the impact of these changes should reassess their thinking on the compensation issue. And the racial component is a good place to begin. An undercurrent, or maybe the driving force of the entire movement, is about the athletes getting their fair share. As it turns out, the optics of college sports, as with many athletic sectors, has African Americans with an extraordinary presence on the field of play. Once again, it's not *all* about race. It's also about simple economics, a partner that we have come to understand is a longtime sidekick to race.

The Amateur Athletic Club of England was the first organization to publicly use the term *amateur*, in 1866. The club defined an amateur as "any gentleman who has never competed in an open competition, or for public money, or for admission money, or with professionals for a prize, public money or admission money, and who has never at any period of his life taught or assisted in the pursuit of athletic exercises as a means of livelihood; nor is a mechanic, artisan, or labourer."[117]

The Amateur Athletic Club sought to give English gentlemen the opportunity to have sports events against each other and not have to compete against professionals. The concepts of amateurism in England were based on class distinctions. These amateur rules revolved around what are referred to as "mechanics clauses" in amateur definitions, such as the one quoted earlier, which maintained that mechanics, artisans, and laborers could not participate in sports as amateurs.[118] There is nothing savory about seeking to preserve rules that have a genesis based in class difference. So the issues that are problematic for African Americans are largely problematic for low-income individuals. The omnipresent issue in this sea change in college sports is about fairness and equality. And the overarching question is this: who should receive what share of revenues from what we know as college sports?

The Legal Segment

A number of legal cases at various stages point to, essentially, the right of student-athletes under NCAA rules to earn money for their athletic prowess. This is money that would go beyond the already allowed room, board, tuition, and educational fees. The cases revolve around intellectual property rights, or the right to revenues for the use of one's likeness and image, and revenues that flow from those marketing rights. The increasing revenues of the power sports— football and basketball—have served as the catalyst for these actions, although it has taken leadership moments from key individuals to move the cases forward.

Division I football and men's basketball are the economic drivers for college sports. In 2010 the NCAA entered into a $10.8 billion agreement with CBS and Turner Broadcasting to broadcast the Division I men's basketball tournament for 14 years; this will channel

$770 million annually to NCAA member colleges. Additionally, there is ESPN's 12-year agreement to broadcast the college football playoff system beginning with the 2014 season for an estimated $500 million per year, and the revenue generated by each of the five major conferences, such as the $314 million in total revenue generated by the Big Ten Conference in 2013 and the $309.6 million collected by the Southeastern Conference (SEC). That SEC number was an increase from $165.9 million in 2009 and just $4.1 million in 1980.[119] Thus the revenue levels have changed dramatically.

The Athletes: Asserting Power in Post-Playing Days

In Chapter 1 I noted the unique role that Magic Johnson played as a former athlete. Ed O'Bannon, the named plaintiff in one of the key cases challenging the current college amateurism structure, was a star basketball player at UCLA. His basketball career and presence in his post-playing days in no way resembled that of Magic Johnson; he was a star college player but less so as a professional afterward. But he did exert a power that no previous former athletic star had chosen to exercise. Years after his playing days were over, he began to take note of the use of his likeness and image in video games. O'Bannon, like other former student-athletes who continued to see their likeness being used, was receiving no income for that use. After conferring with advisors and lawyers, he decided to take action against the NCAA and EA Sports—maker of a number of popular sports-based video games—seeking to halt the use of his likeness and image. The lawsuit was filed in his name. Other suits, similarly brought by student-athletes, were joined with this action. Notably, this was a leadership moment by O'Bannon. Over the years, many had noticed the same phenomenon, but none had taken this assertive action.[120]

In *O'Bannon v. NCAA*,[121] former and current football and basketball student-athletes assert that the NCAA amateurism rules that prevent them from licensing their names and likenesses violate antitrust laws. The plaintiffs sought an injunction—an order from the court that would require the NCAA to change its amateurism rules so as to not preclude such negotiations. In August 2014, after years of litigation, O'Bannon won his injunction, as US district court judge Claudia Wilken ruled, in essence, that college sports is not about amateurism but rather about big business, and players deserve a cut of the revenues. How that revenue will eventually be distributed was, as of this writing, still being sorted out.

As that action and similar ones were moving forward, the other major movement causing rumblings in the college sports world focused on increased compensation generally. This issue has been raised in multiple fashions over the years. A number of legal actions have confronted this issue, with the most dominant in recent times being the Northwestern University unionization effort that was brought before the National Labor Relations Board (NLRB). In that case, a regional office of the NLRB found that scholarship football players at Northwestern University could unionize, because they were technically "employees" of the university, not just students. A group of scholarship football players organized and filed the proper documentation requesting that they attain the right to collectively bargain against Northwestern, as would be the case with any union. The focus of those negotiations would be on hours, wages, and conditions of employment.

That movement has been led by an organization called the National College Players Association (NCPA), led by president Ramogi Huma. Huma, less famous than O'Bannon and many tiers below Magic Johnson, was a linebacker at UCLA and began this unionization movement, as the organization's website states, "after watching the NCAA suspend his All-American teammate Donnie Edwards for accepting groceries when his scholarship money ran out at the end of the month. By the end of his freshman year, Huma realized that, despite the billions of dollars that college athletes generate, the NCAA enforces rules that leave college athletes across the nation without basic protections."[122]

Although the greatest publicity to NCPA has come from this unionization effort, their mission focuses on athlete rights beyond compensation. Increased scholarship dollars are certainly a part of their mission, but so are 10 other key items including ongoing health care, player rights to transfer schools, and a focus on brain trauma risks.[123]

Huma has displayed leadership and courage in moving this effort forward. Similarly, the football players at Northwestern University took what could only be labeled an extraordinary step in seeking unionization. The on-the-ground leader for Northwestern was a former quarterback, Kain Colter, who testified in a way that many found revealing. He maintained that even at Northwestern University, one of the stellar academic institutions in America, playing football was a job and that the members of the football team were more athletes than students. Surprisingly to me and others, at the initial deliberation on this matter by the NLRB, there was a ruling in favor of Huma, Colter, and the Northwestern football players. The ruling stated specifically, "it cannot be said the Employer's scholarship players are 'primarily students.'"[124]

The Northwestern student-athletes, it could be argued, will not be the prime beneficiaries of their own work. I don't think it is too far out of line to say that most of these young men did not come to Northwestern with the highest aspirations of making it to the NFL. I think they also came there understanding that with a Northwestern degree, they would be well positioned for that next step in life beyond football. Certainly student-athletes at schools with less stellar academic reputations and greater post-playing opportunities would benefit by securing these union rights now and greater protections against abuses while in school. That said, the pressure this brings can potentially benefit all.

Increased College Sports Revenues and Equitable Distribution

The issue of revenue distribution equality has become of particular concern as the revenues related to college sports have increased dramatically over the past few years. Apart from the focus of a greater share of the revenues going to student-athletes, however, three other issues make the entire idea of redistributing new college sports revenues much more complicated. Ponder, if you will, these three questions: First, should most of the revenues go to the athletes who generate the most income—men's football and basketball and on some campuses women's basketball? Second, should the revenues from those sports be used to support the nonrevenue sports that are peopled largely by whites?[125] Finally, what is the impact of all of this on Title IX, which exists to guarantee equal opportunity in sports to women? How do we strive for equality, financial and otherwise, as the college landscape changes?

Revenue vs. Nonrevenue Sports

Putting it bluntly, athletes of color dominate in the revenue sports, and while many "nonrevenue," "country club," or "Olympic" sports cannot be labeled as profitable, those programs are revenue losers on a basic financial statement.[126] There are powerful analogies here to how the country was built on the backs of blacks. The idea that blacks, in slavery, provided free labor for nonblacks, is the harshest comparison that many have made.

However, this is not what happens. On most campuses, athletic departments are not making a profit and they are all, to varying degrees, reliant on allocations or subsidies from the central academic institution to survive.[127] So there is a bit of a mixing of the real issues when these two types of sports are set against each other. That is not to say that where there are revenues there could not be a reallocation of spending that directs more of those funds to the interests of student-athletes. Put that way, the issue of what should happen to the nonrevenue sports becomes a bit of a different question.

One prominent country club sport coach once relayed to me an interesting anecdote that provides good perspective on how college sport is not like any other business. This coach focused on donor revenue and development value of the nonrevenue sports. As he noted, some of the biggest donors to his institution did so specifically because they had the opportunity to play a sport that was not football or basketball. The golf team or lacrosse team or field hockey team may not make any money in the stands, in other words. But playing them, for these schools, is in some ways a long-term investment. Similarly, a prominent athletic director reminded me that these nonrevenue sports provide quite a bit of the content for the major conference television deals. "Lacrosse and soccer fill a good bit of that air time."

What Should Be Done?

As the revenues increase at a tremendous rate, opportunities have emerged to do more for student-athletes. While many point purely to increasing the direct cash stipend to student-athletes, others more realistically focus on other benefits that could be developed, such as better and ongoing health care, tuition assistance for those who return to school after pro careers, and better counseling for all regarding the realities of life after sport and how fleeting it all can be. There are more dramatic possibilities, such as formal revenue-sharing plans. These concepts are not without precedent in the academy, where professors have for years shared in revenues from technology created in on-campus laboratories.[128]

A logical response to this, and one we hear often, is this: "If an athlete wants to get paid, he or she should formally turn professional." Much is hidden in that statement. First, there is the assumption that the student-athlete is good enough to reach that level. Second, there is the notion that the college education that would be forfeited wouldn't be missed, and third, related to the first, is that there exists a pro-level league with rules that would allow the athlete to turn pro at an early age. I do not believe that should be encouraged, although it certainly should be allowed. However, few individuals are destined to have a professional career in any sport. The focus of the benefits of participating in athletics should not be on thrusting more youth into the dream world of professionalism.

The most important starting point for thinking about this issue is to understand that the opportunity to become a professional athlete is a rare thing, and the opportunity to become a professional athlete "earlier" than is traditional is rarer still. Less than 1 percent of kids playing virtually any sport in high school find their way to the professional ranks. That is not a viable alternative to more creative options at the collegiate level.[129]

Impacting Gender Equity and Title IX

As was noted, women's sports, apart from women's basketball at a few institutions, do not directly generate profits for their institutions. So how should they be considered in any income redistribution model? Title IX focuses on equal opportunity and funding for women's athletics. That does not mesh with those who want to see the revenues generated staying with those who generate them. A final key issue that emerges in this amateurism and equality space is how opportunities could decline for women should dollars be shifted to these revenue-generating sports. One colleague told me, when I mentioned that the focus of this work would be partially on equality, that the mention of that very word immediately evokes Title IX. But this issue is a complicated one. Should greater equity in terms of the compensation that flows to the revenue generators subtract from the opportunities provided to the Mo'ne Davises of the world? Whatever your thoughts on this, there are those who are adamant on either side of the fence.

The equality that Title IX has brought about should not in any way be impeded and certainly not reversed by any adjustments in the way college sports revenues flow. In fact, I think the complication that the federal act presents, of equal funding and opportunity for all, is the type of difficult issue that must be grappled with if change is to come. Equal funding and equal opportunity in sport is the mandate. Thus, no matter where the desire is to provide greater funding, that funding is likely to be greater still once these additional dollars are tabulated. Doing anything negative here would be yet another round of disrespecting women in sports.

The Depth of Equality

Who is generating that revenue? What is the racial and gender composition of those athletes? Should it matter?

Years ago, initial eligibility rules were the dominant topic in college sports. Proposition 42 and the like were designed to increase the academic performance of student-athletes by making sure they had the right qualifications before coming in. The unintended consequence of that debate was the severe impact such rules would have on the entry of African American athletes. Much of the focus was on a test that many maintained to be culturally biased and not always the best predictor of success. There was no evidence that there was any intent to have a harsher impact on African Americans than other groups, but that was what could at best be labeled an unintended consequence.[130]

Such is the case in the flow of revenues in college sports if one simply steps back and asks: Who could gain substantially from increased revenues? Who is being harmed the most by the absence of revenues? In principle, there is nothing wrong with greater revenues flowing to amateur athletes. It is all about the best use of additional revenues and the logistics and legality of changing the flow of revenues from the status quo with a focus on equality.

Athlete Power Remains Key

The athletes highlighted herein—O'Bannon, Huma, and Magic Johnson in Chapter 1—took their activist stances in their post-playing days. Some of the harshest criticisms I've received in reviews of previous works have been about my longing for an athlete like John Carlos, Tommie Smith, or Muhammad Ali to step up and compel change. My response regarding Carlos and Smith is that we should *all* be looking, anticipating, and hoping for the courageous act to occur at the next leadership moment. It is not the riches that these athletes are acquiring that is so impactful, although it may be at some point; rather, it is how courageous they are when leadership moments emerge.

Power, in its nonmonetary form, has been displayed in some compelling ways over the past several months. LeBron James displayed the power that he possesses in the manner that his free agency decision essentially held even the owners in the NBA captive; it was clear that James had the power to determine both where he would play and for what amount, constrained almost exclusively by the limitations of the collective bargaining agreement. Compellingly, his decision to go home to play in Ohio for the Cleveland Cavaliers displayed a sense of freedom that was reflective of the desires of another African American, former baseball player Curt Flood, who led the fight for free agency decades before.[131]

More powerful, though, was the freedom James displayed in speaking out against the words of Donald Sterling.[132] He did so swiftly and forcefully, in a personal leadership moment, using his power as the greatest player in the game. It was certainly that stance that had an impact on the other players league-wide to recognize the ultimate power they possessed in this moment—the power they held to address the heinous racism displayed by Sterling.[133] He and other athletes showed the same fortitude in joining the protests related to the killing of Eric Garner on Staten Island by wearing "I can't breathe" T-shirts during pregame warm-ups.[134]

The student-athletes at Northwestern also displayed a powerful leadership moment. Student-athletes playing football at Northwestern are some of the least likely to play professionally, and they are also more likely to come from middle-class or upper-class backgrounds. Such was the case with much of the leadership of the civil rights movement led by Dr. Martin Luther King, Jr. Certainly there would be benefit from the goals they sought, but the true beneficiaries were to be those in even more desperate straits—those without the platform, resources, and skills to compel change.

Management Steps

In college sports, in other words, the athlete segment has been the main mover in terms of disrupting the status quo. They have certainly been assisted by the courts, that often powerful segment in the Sports Power Matrix. To me the path forward for management in college sports is twofold.

First, conceptually, a trickle of change has begun. In one instance, the University of Maryland, led by athletic director Kevin Anderson, has it right. Following the O'Bannon ruling and the NCAA structural revisions, the school announced "lifetime scholarships" for their players; in other words, those players have a limitless opportunity to complete their degree, even after their playing days are over.[135] There is much more to do, and the nuance of how this works is less important at this stage than the injection of the proper theme into the discussion. The message is this: no matter how much there is a movement away from the "student-athlete" terminology, and despite court rulings declaring these young men and women as more athletes than students, there is room for college sports leadership to redefine that term in the twenty-first century. There is room to shift the newly available funds to focus on how to truly make college sports something different for those who want the opportunity. Others are doing much that fits with this announcement. Recently the Big 12, Southeastern, Atlantic Coast, Big Ten, and Pacific-12 conferences announced guaranteed four-year scholarships for student-athletes as opposed to the traditional year-to-year renewable scholarships.[136]

Preserving the Student-Athlete and Equal Opportunities

A game-changing moment in my life arrived when I was snatched away from a misdirected and overly football-focused life. Stanford's first black coach, Bill Moultrie, was recruiting a player who would turn out to be his last Stanford recruit: me. As corny as it sounds, and as nonmeaningful as it was in the moment, the only recruiting line he threw at me that I remember today was, "Son, I don't really care if you're All-American on the football field, I want you to be All-American in the classroom."

Well, I achieved neither. But the opportunity was there for a kid whose parents had been successful by attending historically black colleges and professional schools. That is what made it tough for me to grasp what is going on today—that the classroom part of the equation is so difficult for mortal student-athletes to achieve, even if they truly want to do so, because of the intense demands placed on them by the business of college sports. Many observers do not understand how broken the model is and how much the college sports arms race has taken away from the academic experience. That is the real shift that needs to occur—a shift of the dollars to make that happen, to focus on the future health of the athletes and to continue to provide opportunities for the Mo'ne Davises of the world. I do have less concern for men's country club sports. As we have seen so often, it is in those sports where the former wrestler who now runs a hedge fund, for example, will emerge to "save" the program. That may one day be more the case with women's sports. But today is not that day, and sometimes that is the type of outcome that equality requires.

Change is under way in this amateur space. Great caution must be taken regarding who is impacted as change takes place, and vigilance and flexibility are required as change occurs with equality as the key focus.

Conclusion
Where Do We Go From Here?
The Leadership Challenge

Throughout this book I have examined the leadership moments, either positive or negative, taken by stakeholders in various segments of the Sports Power Matrix, including the actions of Adam Silver and Donald Sterling and the thought leadership of current and former athletes such as LeBron James, Ed O'Bannon, and Ramogi Huma as well as sponsors, fans, and the courts. In this, the final chapter, I look at some of the broader issues that leaders must grasp in order to promote the principles of diversity, inclusion, respect, and equality.

The Little Things Are Important

A book that I've come to like and quote a lot is *The White Man's Burden*, by William Easterly. The focus in this work is not on equality, respect, diversity, and inclusion but on another issue entirely: world poverty and hunger, that other small problem that some have sarcastically suggested I tackle. The work does a great job of delving into a dilemma we so often attempt to navigate in so many venues in our lives: is the correct path forward to search for one overall solution or to attack a problem from many different angles in many different ways? The book thoughtfully explains how we often waste our energy seeking a single global solution rather than supporting the multiple smaller ones that we see succeeding—and how we undervalue the small successful steps because we yearn for a massive, immediate overall fix. That sort of solution is not going to be found for world poverty and hunger, nor will it be discovered with these sports matters. As I mentioned, pieces of the puzzle such as a vigilantly reviewed Rooney Rule and the NFL Career Development Symposium are a few examples of small useful steps.

Another example that I have mentioned but not explored provides insight into the depth and breadth that leaders must contemplate. For both employment and vendor opportunities, Major League Baseball (MLB) instituted the Diversity Business Summit.[137] It is described on their website as "the premier sports employment conference and supplier diversity trade fair. This two-day event allows job seekers and entrepreneurs the unique opportunity of meeting with MLB's Clubs at both the Major League and Minor League levels as well as sponsorship partners."[138] The vendor segment of the Sports Power Matrix has not been the primary focus of this work but is an example of the multiple levels on which these issues should be addressed.

The MLB Diversity Business Summit and the NFL Career Development Symposium are simply focused networking for people who otherwise would not have the opportunity to interact with each other. I have attended both. They are different events in terms of attendees. The MLB event is filled with a diverse group of prospective employees and vendors, whereas the NFL event is populated with coaching and league business professionals. But both have similar impacts, featuring extraordinary levels of energy and enthusiasm. The simplicity of that notion should not go without note. Programs that promote networking of diverse groups have succeeded.

Other programs seek to have fans of respective sports pledge to treat each other with respect. This recognition of the influential power that sport can have beyond just its players appears to be growing. Both Major League Soccer (MLS) and the American Hockey League (AHL), for example, have programs allowing their fans to pledge their commitment.[139]

Sports entities have enacted a lot of practices to address these concerns. But a broader dissemination of these best practices is needed. The major sports entities have begun to do a better job of this over the years with programs such as the Sports Diversity and Inclusion Symposium.[140] The first symposium was held in 2012 at NFL headquarters, with subsequent events at the United States Olympic Committee headquarters and in 2014 at The PGA (Professional Golfers' Association) of America offices in Palm Beach, Florida. The focus is the sharing of diversity and inclusion best practices. I helped to coordinate the initial meeting of the group, and at subsequent meetings both attendance by the relevant parties and communication have increased, including periodic conference calls between the annual events.

Throughout I have mentioned youth and school sports programs. The concept is both simple and complex: at the earliest stages of involvement in sport, leaders should incorporate, via curriculum and programming, concepts related to diversity, inclusion, respect, and equality, with a focus on the issues discussed in this book, but— and here is the most difficult part—in a way that is appropriate for each age group. In the same way, the leagues have created programs such as NFL Play 60 or MLB's Reviving Baseball in the Inner Cities (RBI). New York University's Sports and Society program seeks to develop a curriculum that focuses on these issues.[141] The elements of existing programs, such as the Olympic world's SafeSport,[142] as well as entities such as the Positive Coaching Alliance,[143] should be broadly considered. This is also a good place to look at global soccer efforts against racism.

New ideas should be created as well. One sports observer has raised the idea of an independent method for sports entities to determine where they measure in this diversity, inclusion, respect, and equality space relative to other entities. This would require the development of a tool to measure the relevant elements of the enterprise.[144]

The Breadth of Focus

This book does much to explain why taking on the entire package of issues is so crucial. As with *The White Man's Burden*, small successful steps should be positively acknowledged, but their impact on others should also be contemplated and repeated elsewhere for greater impact where appropriate.

Even as this book acknowledges the need to look beyond black and white, I still believe it's worth asking whether the issues of race in this country are distinctive enough to demand a segregated conversation. Society should continue to focus on the descendants of slavery. What is the status of this segment of the population, which formed the basis for all civil rights progress in the United States? Has the focus on wider issues of diversity allowed us to forget what Professor Derrick Bell so eloquently referred to as *The Faces at the Bottom of the Well*?[145] This issue is obviously much bigger than sports, and I hope that leaders from other sectors join in not just contemplating it, but ultimately taking action on it. For me, that enduring lack of focus makes looking at the broader diversity and inclusion issue difficult; the progress of other groups does not make up for the lack of progress among African Americans in this country. Any examination of these issues must be vigilant in keeping that unique dynamic in the frame of analysis.

Why Sport Matters

The Dolphins incident is sort of a *Mona Lisa*; every time you look at it, you easily see something else, some other notion related to this broad space. The mystery of the reality of the interactions. The language related to women. The use of the word *nigger*. Bullying. Interracial interactions. Difference. And so on.

The other undeniable outgrowth of that event was a global recognition of why sport *mattered*. If for no other reason, sport mattered because a single event elevated the conversation about these issues, particularly bullying. It was the same as we saw historically, in a wide range of degrees, with the likes of Jack Johnson, Joe Louis, Jackie Robinson, Althea Gibson, and even Al Campanis and Jimmy the Greek and so many others. In most of those instances and the ones that have been discussed herein—Silver, Magic, Sterling, Snyder, and others—the key question to explore is, "What kind of courage did you display when your leadership moment arrived?"

Yes, sport matters, in the sense that there is still a focus on locker rooms and our fields of play to see what will be done when problems arise. To see if corrective measures occur. To watch for more negative news to hit. To see if lessons emanate from this space that can then be applied elsewhere. Take, for example, the Rooney Rule.

The rule has been discussed for use beyond sports, which is understandable, and there have been debates about expanding it to other leagues within sports, including the English Premier League and global soccer leadership. Efforts have been extensive, for example, to institute a Rooney Rule for college sports coaches and administrators. Richard Lapchick, the sports diversity scholar, has called this the Eddie Robinson rule, after the legendary Grambling State University coach. Another space where it has been advocated is in newsrooms where sport is covered—Lapchick has called that one the Ralph Wiley Rule, after the late great African American sports journalist and author.[146]

What is the real impact of success in sports? I love the tracing of the successful integration of Jackie Robinson into baseball leading to, eventually, the US Supreme Court ruling in favor of racial integration in *Brown v. Board of Education* seven years later. As Earl Warren has often been quoted, "I always turn to the sports pages first, which records people's accomplishments. The front page has nothing but man's failures."[147]

The Multifaceted Diversity Approach

As I mentioned at the outset, I am fortunate enough to work with the National Football League on some of these issues. There, in real time, programming had to be delivered to players, and the programming had to work. The focus in NFL programming for players is on respect, and they approach the programming from many angles. The NFL looks at the inherent inequality of not treating each other with respect, the notion that no one class deserves more or less respect than another.

Michael Useem, whom I mentioned in Chapter 1, urges us to look to leaders who have made the right moves for guidance: "By examining their experience and asking what they did and what they could have done, you can better anticipate what you should do when faced with your own leadership challenges."[148] Useem opens his text with one of my favorite quotes from John F. Kennedy, from *Profiles in Courage*: "To be courageous . . . is an opportunity that sooner or later is presented to all of us."[149] That could not be truer in the sports context with regard to the leaders discussed here.

Don't Overfocus on the Individual

One handy lesson from history is this: do not overly focus on individual wrongdoers. Too much attention can be wasted. This is one of the lessons we are learning again with Donald Sterling. He is *one* person. He, individually, was a problem that is now gone.

I recall being personally infuriated by Marge Schott, the former Cincinnati Reds owner who got into trouble for racist remarks—and seemed entirely unapologetic about it.[150] Dr. Harry Edwards, in words that seem admittedly cruel now, essentially told me that life would take care of her. Years later, she did pass away, and the team's new ownership eventually hired Dusty Baker, an African American, as a manager. Change occurred as the enterprise evolved, and an individual could not stand in the way of change forever. That franchise transition reflects how rapidly change can take place via one mere decision. But even there, eventually Baker was fired by the new ownership. Baker's departure was not as smooth as one would like it to be in that imagined perfect world, and Baker's race was raised by many in evaluating the reasons for his firing.[151] Leadership, in other words, *can* impose policies and support positive change. Progress would bring us to the point where the question regarding race would not be raised.

Sustainable Solutions: The Need for Vigilance

There is a need, however, to stay on alert even where it seems that progress has been made. My wife was a collegiate doubles champion in tennis, and my son is a college tennis player. Years ago we moved to a neighborhood near one of the oldest country clubs in America, featuring grass tennis courts. At some point my wife began a conversation about joining, and we did. This was not without a great deal of thought.

Only three or four black families were members at the time. The club, much like any club, had a lot of bad will with a lot of communities because of prior exclusionary policies. My wife had a horrible memory of the place from junior tennis. She played in a tournament held at the club, and the players were housed together by the region they played for. The black players, however, were all housed together, regardless of the region they were from. This was the early 1970s. Fast-forward forty years later, and my son is the player. He had for years been given a wild-card pass to play in a major tournament there. In his final year, he showed up as agreed and, we believed, the pass, for reasons that are still unexplained, was given to a lower-ranked white kid. After some further investigation, meetings, letters, and calls, we resigned, in a family leadership moment. "Don't sleep" is the vernacular for how vigilant we must be when it comes to this issue.[152]

I mentioned at the outset my detention and cuffing as an accused bank robber. Here I was, the longest-tenured African American professor at the Wharton School of Business, in my late fifties, in a business suit driving midday in suburban Philadelphia. Not only was I stopped by police officers and commanded to exit my vehicle, but I was detained on the street by at least a dozen white police officers and handcuffed, as I was suspected to be a bank robber, an African American, a few decades younger than me. This was nothing unique in the life of African Americans, but a reminder to me of the need for personal vigilance. That day my belief in the level of progress we have made was tempered when I contemplated how many of my white colleagues have had to endure similar incidents, particularly at this stage in life. African Americans endure mega events like this and daily microaggressions. My personal search for respect is to just be treated as are others who are similarly situated.

It was a similar presumption that "all was fine" that led to the disappointing coaching hiring year in the NFL in 2013. The response was a reach back to programming that had originally been successful before the Rooney Rule: self-imposed networking among owners and diverse head coaching and general manager prospects.

Afterword
Avoiding the "Trick Bag"

"The place in which I fit will not exist until I make it."
—James Baldwin[153]

This epigraph from James Baldwin places the obligation on us all, no matter where in the Sports Power Matrix we reside, or even in society as a whole, to seize on our leadership moment. This book has raised questions regarding diversity, inclusion, respect, and equality and provides some framework on how to achieve these goals in an organization and beyond. However, one more element is important to discuss. It is an element that more than one athlete, stretching out a career well beyond the average, will credit when asked how he or she continues to achieve at such a high level: "Hard work." That is the biggest requirement for success in reforming sport and broadly society. This book does not provide all of the answers, but hopefully it provides some framework and points the conversation in the right direction.

In reflecting on the task at hand, I come back to the issue of prioritization. I remember vividly a phrase my elder relatives, led by Aunt Bess, all used with some frequency. "I'm not going to get caught up in that trick bag." To relegate race to just another issue within the diversity "bundle" has the potential to deprive the issue of the focus it should receive.

I know what the term *trick bag* means, but I thought a trip to the online Urban Dictionary might be enlightening: "trick bag: a situation which can lead to a disastrous outcome, normally initiated by someone who dislikes you." That, in a phrase, is my concern of moving away from a race focus to one immersed in diversity, inclusion, respect, and equality.

The overall trick bag to avoid is not only one that loses sight of the race problem but also one that neglects to take into account the multiplicity of equality, respect, diversity, and inclusion issues that exist in today's world. This is the seventh item in the framework set forth at the beginning. It's obviously more complex than these alone, and hopefully the text has provided more context for each:

1. Diversity must be accompanied by inclusion.
2. Addressing these issues requires more than a single action or policy.
3. The actions or policies must be sustained.
4. Leadership must be vigilant regarding the need to revise policies.
5. Negative behavior must be responded to rapidly and decisively but with due process.
6. Where possible, seek to have an impact beyond your enterprise.
7. Race consciousness remains imperative.

When Have We Arrived?

My favorite event during the Super Bowl festivities is the Fritz Pollard Alliance Johnnie Cochran Awards ceremony. On this gala evening, awards are given to individuals who do the most to promote diversity within the NFL. That event is led by John Wooten, whom I mentioned in Chapter 4. When do we know that we have arrived? In Wooten's mind, the answer is this: when the percentages in the front office and league offices equal those on the field of play. It's a commonsense answer. I have contemplated for years what the appropriate percentages are in the sports setting, however, and I've concluded that we get little guidance by looking to those. We must go beyond sheer numbers.

I often ask myself: what is the magic that I anticipated would occur once integration in American society took place? Similarly, when would I know that real and historic progress had been made in sports? Given the nonsports economic plight of African Americans, is it even realistic to target a day when African American owners in our biggest leagues are commonplace? Or will it simply be yet another immeasurable moment when everyone is and feels respected?

As I asked in the introduction, I turn the question back to you: what do you see as the moment of arrival both in sport and beyond?

Acknowledgments

My gratitude first goes out to the consecutive batches of teens and twenty-somethings I have had the opportunity to teach here at Penn every year since 1986. They listen to and critique my ideas and share their own. I also have the opportunity to do the same with a number of scholars around the country, including Dr. Scott Brooks, who was especially giving of his time in reviewing manuscript, as well as Dr. Harry Edwards, the Godfather in this space, whom I am confident I have not completely satisfied, but whose critiques I will always take to heart. Thanks also to Dr. C. Keith Harrison, who commented on an early version; Drew Brown, a scholar, who read an interim draft of this manuscript as well; N. Jeremi Duru, my coauthor on another project, read and commented on a draft as well; Scott Rosner, my foil on many of the issues herein on our SiriusXM Wharton Sports Business radio show and otherwise; and my Wharton Sports Business Initiative colleague, Mori Taheripour, for her helpful comments. Although I did not consult either specifically regarding the book, I have to thank Dr. Todd Boyd for lengthy periodic conversations where we debate these and other topics and Dr. Richard Lapchick for his long work and vigilance in providing the most up-to-date data.

A number of people outside the academy have provided insight, and although I burdened none with reading any part of the manuscript as they are busy doing "the real work," we have spoken at length regarding many of the topics. These include Della Britton Baeza, Wendy Lewis, and Steve Ross and his team.

Big thanks go to Troy Vincent. Over the long haul, the two of us have had intense conversations on how to make a difference and worked on the creation of policies and programming for more than a decade. We have seen each other come to understand how respect, diversity, and inclusion are the paths to success.

I don't want to give social media short shrift either. I have had many exchanges and gained much there. These have included ongoing discussions on a number of topics, live and online, with former teammate John Olenchalk and friend Keith Sparks, especially on NCAA matters. Nevin Caple always finds a way to get back to me to assist in my grasp of diversity issues. My too-infrequent conversation partner Bill Rhoden, when we do talk, always sends me away with something new. More than with anyone else, when I speak with Bill, I pause and wonder if I'm stuck in some civil rights time warp. To those friends I have not named, but you know we've had one or a few of these conversations in person or virtually, thanks to you as well.

Thanks also to the leaders at Wharton Digital Press (later renamed Wharton School Press) for believing in and understanding the need for this book, to Steve Kobrin and Shannon Berning for their work on all aspects of the book, and to Tim Hyland for his editorial and writing contributions.

Finally, thanks to my family, home team, and closest allies in so many of the battles in sport and beyond: Diane, Theresa, and Sam.

Without a doubt, the errors are mine alone, in spite of the input received from all. I know there are those who disagree, and I look forward to hearing from you all so that we can continue to strive to get it right.

Notes

1 John Wooden, *Wooden: A Lifetime of Observations and Reflections On and Off the Court*. http://www.goodreads.com/quotes/175293-although-there-is-no-progress-without-change-not-all-change. Accessed December 2014.

2 https://www.nwhm.org/get-involved/chronicles/women/bess-bolden-walcott/. Accessed December 2014.

3 Kenneth L. Shropshire, *In Black and White: Race and Sports in America*.

4 http://www.newyorker.com/news/news-desk/coward-race. Accessed December 2014.

5 http://www.theatlantic.com/politics/archive/2014/04/dont-sweat-the-microaggressions/360278/. Accessed December 2014.

6 There is a popular culture reference to respect in the movie *Boyz n the Hood* by the father to his son: "Never respect anybody who doesn't respect you back." This concept provides yet another layer of complexity in the respect realm. http://www.imdb.com/video/amazon/vi689545241/. Accessed December 2014.

7 I could go on extensively about the topic, and sport matters that are not used as examples here include the special problems of NASCAR, golf, global cricket, sports agents, and the role of sports apparel firms. I did seek to use examples with the broadest resonance. Regarding some of the issues in soccer see http://espn.go.com/espn/feature/story/_/id/9338962/when-beautiful-game-turns-ugly. Accessed December 2014.

8 http://www.nytimes.com/2009/09/24/sports/basketball/24nets.html?_r=0. Accessed December 2014.

9 As I reviewed the final draft of this manuscript, for example, a controversy erupted regarding St. Louis Rams players protesting in support of the citizens of Ferguson, Missouri. http://www.washingtonpost.com/blogs/early-lead/wp/2014/11/30/rams-protest-ferguson-decision-with-hands-up-gesture-as-they-take-field/. Accessed December 2014.

10 http://www.sportsbusinessdaily.com/Journal/Issues/2014/12/08/Most-Influential/Intro.aspx.

11 W. E. B. DuBois, *The Souls of Black Folks*.

12 Cornel West, *Race Matters*.

13 http://www.coachingmobilityreport.com/uploads/Diversity_Inclusion GoodBusiness_vol1_v2.pdf, p. 3. Accessed December 2014.

14 The most consistent critique of existing studies is that they don't clearly make the causation tie between diversity and positive financial results. http://www.ft.com/cms/s/0/4f4b3c8e-d521-11e3-9187-00144feabdc0.html#axzz3KCuAOrt0. Accessed December 2014.

15 A. Bartlett Giamatti, *Take Time for Paradise: Americans and Their Games*, p. 13.

16 Jim Collins, *Good to Great*.

17 http://www.tidesport.org/index.html. Accessed December 2014.

18 http://bleacherreport.com/articles/1822988-the-rooney-rule-10-years-later-its-worked-usually-and-we-still-need-it. Accessed December 2014.

19 Madden, J. F. (2004), "Differences in the Success of NFL Coaches by Race, 1990–2002," *Journal of Sports Economics* 5(1), 6–19. See also a follow-up study at https://sociology.sas.upenn.edu/sites/sociology.sas.upenn.edu/files/rooneyrulepaper. pdf. Accessed December 2014. For a comprehensive book-length history, see N. Jeremi Duru, *Advancing the Ball: Race, Reformation, and the Quest for Equal Coaching Opportunity in the NFL*.

20 For example, one hire after the symposium was Buffalo Bills general manager Doug Whaley. http://espn.go.com/nfl/story/_/id/9281324/buffalo-bills-promote-doug-whaley-take-gm. Accessed December 2014.

21 John Hope Franklin, *The Color Line: Legacy for the Twenty-First Century*, p. 5.

22 http://www.philly.com/philly/blogs/sports/sixers/Report-Clippers-owner-Donald-Sterling-told-girlfriend-not-to-bring-black-people-to-game. html#KOYZuuZ5JikBfCVD.99. Accessed December 2014.

23 Ibid.

24 http://www.usatoday.com/story/sports/nba/clippers/2014/04/27/donald-sterling-racism-tape-history-los-angeles/8313067/. Accessed December 2014.

25 http://www.usatoday.com/story/sports/nba/clippers/2014/05/29/donald-sterling-steve-ballmer-los-angeles-clippers-sale-2-billion-nba-nancy-armour/9748321/. Accessed December 2014.

26 Shropshire, *In Black and White*, p. 48.

27 Ibid., p. 43.

28 http://www.usatoday.com/story/sports/nba/clippers/2014/04/27/donald-sterling-racism-tape-history-los-angeles/8313067/. Accessed December 2014.

29 Shropshire, *In Black and White*, p. 36.

30 William C. Rhoden, *Forty Million Dollar Slaves: The Rise, Fall, and Redemption of the Black Athlete*, p. 272.

31 http://fivethirtyeight.com/datalab/diversity-in-the-nba-the-nfl-and-mlb/. Accessed December 2014.

32 http://news.yahoo.com/oprah-safe-enough-nba-175000547--politics.html. Accessed December 2014

33 An NBA owner recently told me that even as relatively equal co-owners, only one may be designated to vote at a given meeting on behalf of the franchise.

34 One need only search for the phrase online to see a myriad of references, including videos of preacher's sermons on the theme. I am sure I first heard the usage in church as a child. For an interesting book carrying the title and focused on Latinos, see Rodolfo Rosales, *The Illusion of Inclusion: The Untold Political Story of San Antonio*, http://utpress.utexas.edu/index.php/books/rosill. Accessed December

2014. It is worth noting, too, that proclamations of diversity, without action, are problematic as well. See, for example, a university president proclaiming diversity in her administration and beyond without hiring a single dean of color throughout nearly her first decade in office: http://www.thedp.com/article/2013/01/members-of-the-senior-faculty-of-africana-studies-guess-whos-not-coming-to-dinner. Accessed December 2014.

35 http://transcripts.cnn.com/TRANSCRIPTS/1405/06/csr.01.html. Accessed December 2014.

36 Michael Useem, *The Leadership Moment*.

37 Ibid, p. 3.

38 https://www.youtube.com/watch?v=OJ_BsWrTQZo. Accessed December 2014.

39 Ibid.

40 Shropshire, *In Black and White*, pp. 21–24.

41 http://www.usatoday.com/story/sports/nba/2014/04/28/cuban-ousting-donald-sterling-slippery-slope/8442461/. Accessed December 2014.

42 http://www.nba.com/hawks/copy-bruce-levensons-email. Accessed December 2014.

43 http://www.usatoday.com/story/sports/nba/clippers/2014/08/12/los-angeles-clippers-sale-steve-ballmer-donald-sterling-nba/13952797/. Accessed December 2014.

44 http://www.tmz.com/2014/04/27/donald-sterling-new-audio-released-clippers-black-people/. Accessed December 2014.

45 Ibid.

46 http://www.nytimes.com/1992/07/09/sports/football-judge-strikes-upshaw-attack.html. Accessed December 2014.

47 http://espn.go.com/nba/story/_/id/11868612/nba-owners-expendable-players union-chief-michele-roberts-says. Accessed December 2014.

48 http://www.latimes.com/local/lanow/la-me-ln-state-farm-carmax-donald-sterling-clippers-20140428-story.html. Accessed December 2014.

49 http://www.law360.com/articles/560129/donald-sterling-sues-nba-wife-to-block-2b-clippers-sale. Accessed December 2014.

50 http://transcripts.cnn.com/TRANSCRIPTS/1405/06/csr.01.html; http://insidetv. ew.com/2014/05/06/msnbc-apology-cinco-de-mayo-segment/. Accessed December 2014.

51 See http://time.com/3329351/ray-rice-timeline/ for a timeline of the entire event. Accessed December 2014.

52 Ibid.

53 http://www.sbnation.com/nfl/2014/5/23/5744964/ray-rice-arrest-assault-statement-apology-ravens. Accessed December 2014. With that the league announced new, stiffer sanctions for domestic violence. http://www.sbnation.com/ nfl/2014/8/28/6079465/nfl-announces-new-domestic-violence-policy. Accessed December 2014.

54 http://bleacherreport.com/articles/2190975-video-of-ray-rice-incident-with-wife-janay-palmer-leaked-by-tmz. Accessed December 2014.

55 http://www.imdb.com/title/tt0255819/; https://www.youtube.com/
watch?v=iwnbD2Jfkjk. Accessed December 2014.
56 http://www.si.com/nfl/2014/12/01/janay-rice-today-show-interview?xid=nl_siextra.
Accessed December 2014.
57 http://www.thewrap.com/keith-olbermann-blasts-nfl-roger-goodell-over-ray-
rice-incident-video/. Accessed December 2014. See also http://www.nytimes.
com/2014/11/30/sports/football/roger-goodell-has-32-nfl-owners-in-his-corner-
for-now.html?_r=0, noting the media deals and extraordinary revenues Goodell
has negotiated for league owners. Accessed December 2014.
58 http://www.usatoday.com/story/sports/nfl/2014/11/28/ray-rice-suspension-
overturned-nfl-appeal/19182415/; http://i.usatoday.net/sports/nfl/2014-11-28-
Ray-Rice-appeal.pdf. Accessed December 2014.
59 http://www.si.com/college-football/2014/10/07/florida-sexual-assault-charges-
matt-mauk. Accessed December 2014.
60 http://nomore.org/nflplayerspsa/. Accessed December 2014.
61 See http://www.cnn.com/2014/09/15/us/nfl-goodell-domestic-violence/index.html.
Accessed December 2014. Even that group was criticized for its lack of diversity,
even though at least two African American female NFL employees were engaged
on the issues; see http://espn.go.com/nfl/story/_/id/11542482/the-black-women-
roundtable-criticizes-nfl-hiring-female-consultants. Accessed December 2014.
62 http://www.usatoday.com/story/sports/nba/hawks/2014/09/07/bruce-levenson-
racist-email-atlanta-owner-sell-team/15241591/. Accessed December 2014.
63 http://www.cnn.com/2014/09/17/us/adrian-peterson-child-abuse-charges/index.
html. Accessed December 2014.
64 http://money.cnn.com/2014/09/15/news/adrian-peterson-vikings-radisson/index.
html. Accessed December 2014.
65 Ibid.
66 http://www.ncai.org/attachments/policypaper_
mijapmouwdbjqftjayzqwlqldrwzvsyfakbwthpmatcoroyolpn_ncai_harmful_mascots_
report_ending_the_legacy_of_racism_10_2013.pdf. Accessed December 2014.
67 Ibid.
68 http://www.thedailybeast.com/articles/2014/06/30/pancakes-and-pickaninnies-the-
saga-of-sambo-s-the-racist-restaurant-chain-america-once-loved.html#. Accessed
December 2014.
69 http://www.nytimes.com/1989/01/27/business/colgate-to-rename-a-toothpaste.html.
Accessed December 2014.
70 See for example the support of the name Fighting Sioux related to the University of
North Dakota, http://www.washingtonmonthly.com/college_guide/blog/fighting_
sioux_will_fight_no_m.php.
71 http://ap-gfkpoll.com/featured/our-latest-story-2. Accessed December 2014.
72 Ibid.
73 http://www.annenbergpublicpolicycenter.org/downloads/political_communication/
naes/2004_03_redskins_09-24_pr.pdf. Accessed December 2014.

74 http://ap-gfkpoll.com/featured/our-latest-story-2. Accessed December 2014.
75 http://espn.go.com/nfl/story/_/id/9772653/president-obama-washington-redskins-legitimate-concerns. Accessed December 2014.
76 http://www.washingtonpost.com/opinions/washington-post-editorials-will-no-longer-use-redskins-for-the-local-nfl-team/2014/08/22/1413db62-2940-11e4-958c-268a320a60ce_story.html. Accessed December 2014.
77 http://www.washingtonpost.com/blogs/dc-sports-bog/wp/2014/09/02/espn-poll-58-percent-of-nfl-players-say-redskins-should-keep-their-name/. Accessed December 2014.
78 http://www.usatoday.com/story/sports/nfl/redskins/2013/05/09/washington-redskins-daniel-snyder/2148127/. Accessed December 2014.
79 http://www.washingtonexaminer.com/redskins-poll-blacks-democrats-women-support-name/article/2553663. Accessed December 2014.
80 http://www.washingtonpost.com/local/letter-from-washington-redskins-owner-dan-snyder-to-fans/2013/10/09/e7670ba0-30fe-11e3-8627-c5d7de0a046b_story.html. Accessed December 2014.
81 http://ap-gfkpoll.com/featured/our-latest-story-2. Accessed December 2014.
82 http://www.washingtonpost.com/blogs/football-insider/wp/2013/02/14/bruce-allen-no-plans-to-change-redskins-name/. Accessed December 2014.
83 http://www.usatoday.com/story/sports/nfl/redskins/2013/06/11/washington-redskins-congress-roger-goodell/2412809/. Accessed December 2014.
84 Ibid.
85 http://ap-gfkpoll.com/featured/our-latest-story-2. Accessed December 2014.
86 http://online.wsj.com/articles/SB10001424052702304655304579548121845954320. Accessed December 2014.
87 The numbers are particularly striking at the high school level. See http://blogs.marketwatch.com/thetell/2013/10/11/500-high-schools-use-redskins-indians-or-braves-as-team-name/. Accessed December 2014.
88 http://www.nytimes.com/2014/06/19/sports/football/us-patent-office-cancels-redskins-trademark-registration.html?_r=0. Accessed December 2014.
89 http://www.forbes.com/nfl-valuations/. Accessed December 2014.
90 http://www.washingtonpost.com/news/fancy-stats/wp/2014/06/18/how-much-it-would-cost-to-change-the-redskins-name/. Accessed December 2014. That is truly a nominal amount for a franchise that is worth in the neighborhood of $2 billion with annual revenues approaching $375 million. See the current Forbes franchise valuation at http://www.forbes.com/nfl-valuations/list/. Accessed December 2014.
91 Merchandise sales went up more than 75 percent with the name change. See http://charlotte.twcnews.com/content/news/713377/economic-boost-arrives-with-sports-team-name-change/. Accessed December 2014.
92 Charles K. Ross, *Outside the Lines: African Americans and the Integration of the National Football League*, pp. 81–98.
93 http://m.bizjournals.com/milwaukee/news/2014/09/30/99-9-of-fedex-shareholders-ok-with-redskins.html?r=full. Accessed December 2014.

94 Similar to sponsor pressure in the case of the University of North Dakota, a donor threatened to terminate a donation if the Fighting Sioux name was dropped, http://espn.go.com/college-sports/story/_/id/8429126/ncaa-allows-most-north-dakota-sioux-logos-stay. Accessed December 2014.

95 http://i.usatoday.net/sports/nfl/miami-dolphins-ted-workplace-conduct-report.pdf. Accessed December 2014. The *Report to the National Football League Concerning Issues of Workplace Conduct at the Miami Dolphins*, by Theodore V. Wells, Jr., Brad S. Karp, Bruce Birenboim, and David W. Brown, commonly referred to as the Wells Report, is the most complete, publicly available insight on this event, but even after reviewing it thoroughly one still cannot confidently understand exactly what transpired and why, regardless of what other commentators may have set forth.

96 Ibid.

97 Ibid.

98 Ibid., pp. 7–8.

99 http://www.usnews.com/news/articles/2014/02/26/nfl-may-penalize-use-of-the-n-word-on-the-field. Accessed December 2014.

100 http://espn.go.com/nfl/story/_/id/10500657/nfl-expected-penalize-players-using-racial-slurs-games. Accessed December 2014.

101 Wells Report, Appendix B.

102 Wells Report, p. 48.

103 Ibid.

104 http://www.advocate.com/commentary/2014/10/27/op-ed-why-michael-sam-saga-matters. Accessed December 2014.

105 http://www.wtt.com/. Accessed December 2014.

106 http://espn.go.com/womens-college-basketball/story/_/id/7219014/penn-state-nittany-lions-again-deficient-leadership. Accessed December 2014.

107 http://www.advocate.com/sports/2014/11/19/jason-collins-announces-retirement. Accessed December 2014.

108 Probably of greatest note was the negative commentary over social media when Michael Sam was drafted. See http://espn.go.com/nfl/draft2014/story/_/id/10915408/2014-nfl-draft-miami-dolphins-gm-disappointed-don-jones-tweet-regards-michael-sam. Accessed December 2014.

109 http://www.csmonitor.com/Business/2014/1030/Tim-Cook-comes-out-7-milestones-for-gay-rights-in-the-corporate-world/Rick-Welts. Accessed December 2014.

110 http://www.si.com/more-sports/2014/08/20/mone-davis-taney-little-league-world-series. Accessed December 2014.

111 http://sports.yahoo.com/news/little-league-ceo—we-ll-consider-compensating-players-in-future-053214653.html. Accessed December 2014.

112 http://www.usatoday.com/story/sports/college/2014/10/22/mone-davis-ncaa-amateur-status-eligibility-chevrolet-commercial-uconn-huskies-llws/17702519/. Accessed December 2014.

113 Ibid.

114 David C. Young, *The Olympic Myth of Greek Amateur Athletics*, p. 7.

115 Ibid., p. 1.

116 http://www.washingtonpost.com/sports/colleges/ncaa-board-of-directors-approves-autonomy-for-big-5-conference-schools/2014/08/07/807882b4-1e58-11e4-ab7b-696c295ddfd1_story.html. Accessed December 2014.

117 E. Glader, *Amateurism and Athletics*, p. 100.

118 Ibid.

119 Brad Wolverton, "NCAA Agrees to $10.8 Billion Deal to Broadcast Its Men's Basketball Tournament," *Chronicle of Higher Education*, April 22, 2010; "ESPN to Broadcast College Football Playoffs for 12 Years Starting in 2014," NCAA.com, November 21, 2012, http://www.ncaa.com/news/football/article/2012-11-21/espn-broadcast-college-football-playoffs-12-years-starting-2014 (accessed December 2014); Steve Berkowitz, "Big Ten Still Leads Leagues in College Sports Revenue," *USA Today*, May 16, 2014.

120 http://www.usatoday.com/story/sports/college/2014/08/08/ed-obannon-antitrust-lawsuit-vs-ncaa/13801277/. Accessed December 2014.

121 http://i.usatoday.net/sports/!Investigations-and-enterprise/OBANNONRULING.pdf. Accessed December 2014.

122 http://www.ncpanow.org/about/about-the-ncpa-president. Accessed December 2014.

123 http://www.ncpanow.org/about/mission-goals. Accessed December 2014.

124 National Labor Relations Board Region 13, Case 13-RC-121359 (March 26, 2014). http://www.cnn.com/2014/images/03/26/Decision_and_Direction_of_Election.pdf. Accessed December 2014.

125 There is an interesting power of language use at work in how one refers to the nonrevenue sports. *Nonrevenue* sports is probably the most neutral term, *Olympic sports* is the most positive term, and *country club* sports is probably the most probing and illuminating term. *Nonrevenue* is probably the most accurate, as many of the sports beyond basketball and football are present neither at the Olympics nor in country clubs. However, *nonrevenue* is not literally accurate either. Programs and concessions are often sold at these events, and that income would constitute revenue even if not profit.

126 Ibid.

127 http://www.usatoday.com/story/sports/college/2013/05/07/ncaa-finances-subsidies/2142443/. Accessed December 2014.

128 A former athletics administrator friend of mine sets this concept forward at every opportunity. For more on the technology transfer concept, see http://chronicle.com/article/University-Inventions-Earned/133972/. Accessed December 2014. The analogy is much like that for invented technology, except that if not for the athletes' skills, the revenue would not flow to the university.

129 The following chart shows the probability of competing in athletics beyond high school—both college and professionally. These percentages are based on estimated data. http://www.ncaa.org/about/resources/research/probability-competing-beyond-high-school. Accessed December 2014.

Student-Athletes	Men's Basketball	Women's Basketball	Football	Baseball	Men's Ice Hockey	Men's Soccer
High School Student-Athletes	538,676	433,120	1,086,627	474,791	35,198	410,982
High School Senior Student-Athletes	153,907	123,749	310,465	135,655	10,057	117,423
NCAA Student-Athletes	17,984	16,186	70,147	32,450	3,964	23,365
NCAA Freshman Roster Positions	5,138	4,625	20,042	9,271	1,133	6,676
NCAA Senior Student-Athletes	3,996	3,597	15,588	7,211	881	5,192
NCAA Student-Athletes Drafted	46	32	254	678	7	101
Percent High School to NCAA	3.3%	3.7%	6.5%	6.8%	11.3%	5.7%
Percent NCAA to Professional	1.2%	0.9%	1.6%	9.4%	0.8%	1.9%
Percent High School to Professional	0.03%	0.03%	0.08%	0.50%	0.07%	0.09%

130 Shropshire, *In Black and White*, pp. 103–127.

131 http://www.usatoday.com/story/sports/nba/cavaliers/2014/07/11/lebron-james-return-cleveland-cavaliers-contract-miami-heat/12444643/. Accessed December 2014.

132 http://espn.go.com/nba/truehoop/miamiheat/story/_/id/10844906/lebron-james-no-room-donald-sterling-nba. Accessed December 2014.

133 Beyond sport there is what seems to be an increase in athlete activism, particularly in race-related matters. This has included commentary led by LeBron James on the Trayvon Martin and Michael Brown cases, http://espn.go.com/nba/story/_/id/11938106/lebron-james-others-comment-ferguson-decision. Accessed December 2014.

134 http://espn.go.com/nba/story/_/id/12001456/lebron-james-kyrie-irving-cleveland-cavaliers-kevin-garnett-deron-williams-brooklyn-nets-wear-breathe-shirt-reference-eric-garner. Accessed December 2014.

135 http://articles.baltimoresun.com/2014-08-19/sports/bal-maryland-guaranteed-scholarships-for-student-athletes-20140819_1_scholarship-program-sasho-cirovski-new-program. Accessed December 2014.

136 http://www.si.com/college-football/2014/12/01/big-12-power-5-conference-multi-year-scholarships?xid=nl_siextra. Accessed December 2014.
http://www.nytimes.com/2014/10/28/sports/pac-12-guarantees-4-year-scholarships.html?_r=0. Accessed December 2014.

137 http://mlb.mlb.com/mlb/official_info/mlb_official_info_diverse.jsp?content=summit. Accessed December 2014.

138 Ibid.

139 http://www.mlssoccer.com/mlsworks/dontcrosstheline and http://youcanplayproject.org/page/s/take-the-captains-challenge. Accessed December 2014.

140 http://www.pgalinks.com/diversity/symposium.cfm. Accessed December 2014.

141 http://nyusportsandsociety.org/. Accessed December 2014.

142 http://training.safesport.org/. Accessed December 2014.

143 http://www.positivecoach.org/. Accessed December 2014.

144 One possibility is something like B Labs, which measures and certifies companies as having positive social and environmental qualities. See http://www.bcorporation.net/. Accessed December 2014. This is greater rigor in the same spirit in which Dr. Richard Lapchick has issued the Racial Report Card periodically evaluating the diversity of leagues with a letter grade. http://www.tidesport.org/racialgenderreportcard.html. Accessed December 2014.

145 Derrick Bell, *The Faces at the Bottom of the Well.*

146 There is even legislation calling for the use of a similar rule in corporate America. See http://www.theroot.com/articles/politics/2014/08/bet_founder_bob_johnson_touts_a_new_corporate_sector_rooney_rule.html. Accessed December 2014.

147 http://www.brainyquote.com/quotes/quotes/e/earlwarren106227.html#g3xep6uGMhOFhs9F.99. Accessed December 2014.

148 Useem, *The Leadership Moment*, p. 3.

149 Ibid.

150 http://articles.latimes.com/1996-05-12/sports/sp-3360_1_marge-schott. Accessed December 2014.

151 http://www.si.com/mlb/strike-zone/2013/10/04/cincinnati-reds-fire-dusty-baker; http://blacktopxchange.com/2013/10/04/dusty-baker-race-and-the-lack-of-appreciation-of-a-black-baseball-manager/. Accessed December 2014.

152 In spite of that moment, and to show my impartiality with regard to country club sports, my son ended up playing tennis at Northwestern and my daughter squash at Stanford. A bigger issue, but personal as well, was referee Mike Carey's decision not to work Redskin's games due to the name. http://www.si.com/nfl/2014/08/20/mike-carey-washington-redskins-games. Accessed December 2014.

153 http://www.newyorker.com/magazine/2009/02/09/another-country. Accessed December 2014.

Index

About the Author

Kenneth L. Shropshire is the David W. Hauck Professor at the Wharton School of the University of Pennsylvania, the faculty director of its Wharton Sports Business Initiative, and Professor of Africana Studies. Shropshire joined the Wharton faculty in 1986 and specializes in sports business and law.

His consulting roles have included a wide variety of projects including work for the NCAA, Major League Baseball, the National Football League, and the United States Olympic Committee. In 2000, the mayor of Philadelphia appointed Shropshire to chair Philadelphia's stadium site selection committee and, later, assist on projects focused on future Philadelphia bids for the Olympic Games. He currently leads the research efforts of the Major League Baseball On-Field Diversity Task Force. He is developing a nonprofit focused on respect in sports and beyond at the behest of Miami Dolphins owner Stephen Ross. Shropshire also serves as the academic director of Wharton's Business Management and Entrepreneurship Program for NFL players focusing on their transition away from the game. He has served as an arbitrator for the NFL Players Association (NFLPA) and USA Track & Field (USATF).

Shropshire hosts Wharton Sports Business Show on SiriusXM Radio and teaches the Coursera course *The Global Business of Sports*, to 30,000 global students. He is also special counsel to the global law firm Duane Morris LLP.

He is a founder and member of the board of directors of the Valley Green Bank in Philadelphia. He serves on the board of Moelis & Co. He is also a former president of the Sports Lawyers Association, the largest such organization in the world, and program chair of the ABA Forum Committee, Sports Law Section.

He earned an undergraduate degree in economics from Stanford University and his law degree from Columbia University. He then joined the law firm of Manatt, Phelps, Rothenberg and Tunney in Los Angeles and later served as an executive with the Los Angeles Olympic Organizing Committee.

The most recent of his ten books are *Negotiate Like the Pros: A Top Sports Negotiator's Lessons for Making Deals, Building Relationships and Getting What You Want,* and *Being Sugar Ray: The Life of America's Greatest Boxer and First Celebrity Athlete.* His works include the foundational books *In Black and White: Race and Sports in America, The Business of Sports,* and *The Business of Sports Agents.*

To learn about other books by Kenneth L. Shropshire, please visit www.KennethShropshire.com.

**WHARTON
SCHOOL
PRESS**

About Wharton School Press

Wharton School Press, the book publishing arm of The Wharton School of the University of Pennsylvania, was established to inspire bold, insightful thinking within the global business community.

Wharton School Press publishes a select list of award-winning, bestselling, and thought-leading books that offer trusted business knowledge to help leaders at all levels meet the challenges of today and the opportunities of tomorrow. Led by a spirit of innovation and experimentation, Wharton School Press leverages groundbreaking digital technologies and has pioneered a fast-reading business book format that fits readers' busy lives, allowing them to swiftly emerge with the tools and information needed to make an impact. Wharton School Press books offer guidance and inspiration on a variety of topics, including leadership, management, strategy, innovation, entrepreneurship, finance, marketing, social impact, public policy, and more.

Wharton School Press also operates an online bookstore featuring a curated selection of influential books by Wharton School faculty and Press authors published by a wide range of leading publishers.

To find books that will inspire and empower you to increase your impact and expand your personal and professional horizons, visit *wsp.wharton.upenn.edu.*

UNIVERSITY *of* PENNSYLVANIA

About The Wharton School

Founded in 1881 as the world's first collegiate business school, the Wharton School of the University of Pennsylvania is shaping the future of business by incubating ideas, driving insights, and creating leaders who change the world. With a faculty of more than 235 renowned professors, Wharton has 5,000 undergraduate, MBA, Executive MBA, and doctoral students. Each year 18,000 professionals from around the world advance their careers through Wharton Executive Education's individual, company-customized, and online programs. More than 99,000 Wharton alumni form a powerful global network of leaders who transform business every day.

For more information, *visit www.wharton.upenn.edu.*